FLOUR LAB

An At-Home Guide to Baking
with Freshly Milled Grains

ADAM LEONTI

WITH **KATIE PARLA**

FOREWORD BY **MARC VETRI**

Photographs by Andrew Thomas Lee

CLARKSON POTTER/PUBLISHERS
NEW YORK

This book is dedicated to the Leonti family, Marc Vetri, Katie Parla, and everyone who helped along the way.

Published in the United States by Clarkson Potter/Publishers,
an imprint of Random House, a division of Penguin Random House
LLC, New York.
clarksonpotter.com

CLARKSON POTTER is a trademark and POTTER with colophon is a
registered trademark of Penguin Random House LLC.

Library of Congress Cataloging-in-Publication Data
Names: Leonti, Adam, author. | Parla, Katie, author.
Title: Flour lab: an at-home guide to baking with freshly milled grains /
Adam Leonti with Katie Parla.
Description: First edition. | New York: Clarkson Potter/Publishers,
2018.
Identifiers: LCCN 2018004040 (hardcover) | LCCN 2018020313 (ebook) |
ISBN 9781524760960 (hardcover) | ISBN 9781524760977 (ebook)
Subjects: LCSH: Flour. | Baking. | LCGFT: Cookbooks.
Classification: LCC TX393 (ebook) | LCC TX393 .L48 2018 (print) |
DDC 641.3/31—dc23
LC record available at https://lccn.loc.gov/2018004040.

ISBN 978-1-5247-6096-0
Ebook ISBN 978-1-5247-6097-7

Printed in China

Book design by Stephanie Huntwork
Cover photographs by Andrew Thomas Lee

10 9 8 7 6 5 4 3 2 1

First Edition

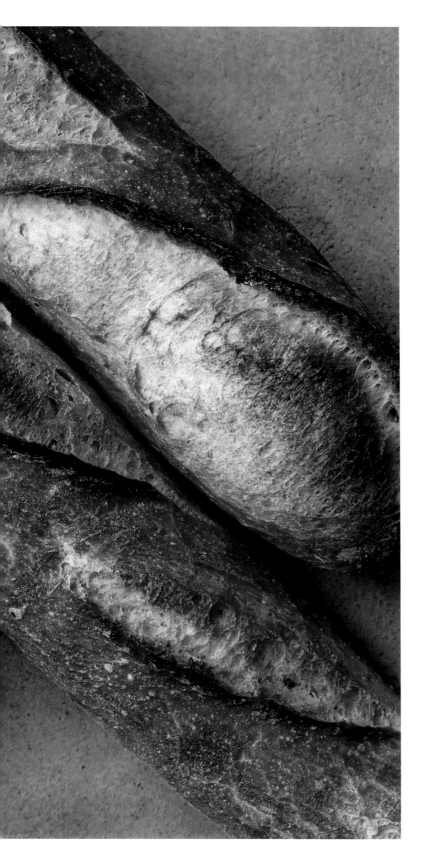

CONTENTS

FOREWORD BY MARC VETRI

It was a random trip to a seed conference at Stone Barns in the fall of 2013 that began my unexpected journey into the world of wheat. A seed was planted (no pun intended) by Dr. Stephen Jones, a wheat breeder from Washington State University, who gave a captivating talk on the flavor in wheat. Adam and I were set to depart on a research trip to Italy to visit artisan pasta makers up and down the boot two days later.

At that time, Adam had been working with me for eight years. When I invited him to join me at this conference, he was curious. Adam was always curious. On mornings in the restaurant, he was always sitting at table six reading a food history book—always opting for culture rather than a cookbook full of photography. He seemed most intrigued by the cuisine of the seventeenth century, as if he wanted to bring it back to life with a more modern approach. One could say his cooking style was an anachronism in the modern restaurant world.

But this connection to the past is why his response was curiosity. Wheat resonated with Adam on an elemental level: there is nothing more pure to work with than a grain of wheat. There's nothing to hide behind, no smoke and mirrors—it's a true empty canvas for an artisan to experiment with.

We were confronted with this and other concepts at the seed conference at Stone Barns. Plant breeders and grain scientists hosted discussions for an audience of world-renowned chefs—Ferran Adrià, Michel Bras, Enrique Olvera, and Gaston Acurio to name a few. Our host, chef Dan Barber, had brought together these influential minds with the goal of changing our minds about the possibilities grains could provide in the kitchen. I know I speak for my colleagues when I say our minds were blown.

The people with whom I work inspire me to search and dig deep, and Adam was no exception. I was certainly intrigued by wheat, but back at the restaurant it was Adam who pushed the limits and boundaries. We had already started an upstairs private dining/kitchen renovation and Adam helped transform part of that space into a sort of lab where he could research grains and milling. He spent hours up there honing his milling techniques and perfecting his recipes for pasta, bread, and pastries made from freshly milled flour.

Flour Lab is an obvious step in Adam's quest to bring fresh-milled flour to the world. The methods discussed here make the concepts easy for a reader to understand. This book is less about a cool new kitchen tool or a single bread recipe than it is about helping you understand that, after technique, the only way to make better, more flavorful bread is to start with better, more flavorful wheat.

Adam spent about ten years with me at Vetri. He's a complete original and this book is an amazing representation of how he takes something that he is passionate about, dissects it, and reduces it to its basic core principle. I believe you will appreciate Adam's view of how the wheat and grain industry has evolved over the last 150 years. And even more than that, you will love milling fresh grains in your home and learning how to transform them into flour and ultimately into everything you already love to cook and bake.

INTRODUCTION

Before I say anything else, I should probably reveal my sole reason for writing this book: *Food made with freshly milled flour is better for your health, the environment, and flavor. I want everyone to start using it.*

Cooking and baking with freshly milled flour is a real passion and has become a significant part of what fuels me as a chef. One of the greatest aspects of working with food is that if you listen to the ingredients, they will tell you how to use them. I don't mean this in some wacky, whimsical way, but in the most practical sense. If you pick up an apple and it's underripe, use its texture to your advantage: slice it thinly and toss it in a salad. Give an overripe apple over to its natural evolution and mash it into jam or bake it into a pie. And if it's perfectly ripe, just take a bite. I'm a firm believer that ingredients should dictate the menu, not the cook preparing it. I apply the same reasoning to wheat. Red Fife and other hard wheat varieties are adapted for making big, airy loaves of bread, while soft wheats like Sonora, which was historically and famously used to make super large tortillas in the Mexican state of Sonora, are best for pastries and cakes. Some wheat varieties are all-around performers and can do almost anything, but it's up to the baker or cook to coax and tame their versatile characteristics.

It is so personally rewarding for me to introduce people to how good freshly milled flour is and how it can be harnessed. Seeing someone's face light up when they try a slice of my fresh-milled durum sourdough bread, or hearing that they feel nourished from eating a whole wheat croissant I have baked—that's what drives me.

If you're skeptical, remember that it wasn't so long ago that buying organic food was considered highbrow and unnecessary. I remember early in my career seeing a celebrated chef yell at his sous-chef for buying organic vegetables because they were considerably more expensive. At the time, his frustration seemed rational. But before long, opinions changed, and a greater knowledge and understanding led us to accept that buying chemical-free produce was responsible food sourcing and the right thing to do for our bodies.

I'm a chef. I feed people. The word "restaurant" derives from the French "to restore to a former state," and I feel strongly that if people trust me with their time, money, and calories, I have a duty to nourish them to the best of my abilities. I am also an enthusiastic teacher and I love to share recipes and techniques with home cooks and professionals alike, so I am excited to share my approach to using flour with you. Throughout this book, we will explore the wonderful world of milling, how to source grains for milling at home, and how to approach purchasing fresh flour directly from a mill. We'll get into the intricacies of working with fresh flour, and discuss how the characteristics of different grains work alone or in unison to create flavor and structure for bread, pasta, pizza, and pastry. With its collection of simple and adaptable recipes that highlight just how good *true* whole-grain cooking and baking can be, I hope this book changes the way you think about cooking and ingredients for good.

Food made with freshly milled flour is better for your health, the environment, and flavor.

THE
STATE
OF
GRAIN

MY JOURNEY TO FRESHLY MILLED FLOUR

Over a career that has spanned twenty years, I have been fortunate enough to work with some very experienced and generous people. Many of them helped illuminate a whole new culinary approach for me. These lessons, learned throughout my time in the restaurant business, have resulted in a continuing journey into the exploration of whole grains and milling. Here's how I got to where I am now.

GROWING UP

My mom grew up in a town in upstate New York with a population of 6,000 people. She made her own clothes, hunted for her food, and milled her own flour. In other words, she is a complete badass. That era was the 1980s and whole, organic foods were in fashion, but so were kitchen appliances. Home milling wasn't super unusual. She would make dough with her freshly milled flour, pop it in a bread machine, and this delicious loaf would come out. I thought it was magic. I spent a lot of time in the kitchen with her and with other members of my family.

When I was fourteen, I got my first job at the Italian Heritage Center, a members-only club in Portland, Maine. It was a huge place with multiple banquet halls, all named after Italian heroes like Columbus and Galileo. It was the ideal spot for a young and inexperienced Italian American kid like me to learn the ropes of the restaurant business. And it was endlessly entertaining seeing all these "Italian" New Englanders with thick Maine accents scarfing down spaghetti and meatballs as if they were in the old country. The food was your standard Italian American fare featuring the greatest hits like veal piccata, lemon chicken, and eggplant Parmesan. We made all the classics. From the moment I started in the kitchen, I was obsessed.

After four years at the Heritage Center—and after graduating from high school—I needed to find a job that paid me more than seven bucks an hour. A cook I knew there offered to get me a gig with his dad working on a ferryboat. The line served Casco Bay, shuttling people and cargo from the Portland mainland to the surrounding islands.

I loved being on the water every day, and the deckhand banter was even more of a sport than cooking, but despite the significant increase in wages, it wasn't long before I missed being around food. While still working on the ferry, I took a part-time job at Henry VIII, a very popular spot that specialized in a variety of roast beef sandwiches. Each day I would prep forty pounds of top round beef that would cook overnight, low and slow at 140°F, in an Alto-Shaam oven. As simple as the concept was, the preparations were diverse, and before long I was learning how to make hollandaise sauce, mushroom ragù, soups, and chutneys.

The owner, Bruce Rascher, was an interesting dude. He had been raised in France, attended hotel school in Switzerland, and cooked all over the world. To this day I have no idea why he opened a sandwich shop in Portland—he was a properly trained restaurateur and could have made it anywhere. I owe Bruce so much for my appreciation of food, and for encouraging me to go to culinary school. He had a connection at The Restaurant

School at Walnut Hill College in Philadelphia, and after one phone call and Bruce's letter of recommendation, I was on my way.

**PHILADELPHIA
TO ITALY . . .
AND BACK**

I began culinary school in early 2004 with classes five days a week from 6 a.m. until 2 p.m. I arrived feeling pretty confident in the kitchen, but I quickly realized I had a lot to learn. Yes, I made a mean chicken parm, but I had absolutely no idea about anything other than the dishes I'd cooked at my first two jobs.

Knife skills, building sauces, butchering meats, and the basic etiquette of working in a kitchen brigade were all disciplines I would soon employ. I was gaining an essential culinary vocabulary that would be a requirement if I wanted to land a job in a city kitchen, which I ultimately did: Barclay Prime, Striped Bass, Le Bec-Fin, and the Fountain Restaurant at the Four Seasons Hotel—all in Philadelphia.

After having cooked in these top joints and honed my culinary chops, I was feeling pretty proud of myself for becoming part of the Philly restaurant scene. Wanting to impress my girlfriend at the time, I made a reservation at a place called Vetri. I was curious about this tiny spot on Spruce Street that had gained national attention by being named the best Italian restaurant in the country by Alan Richman, the intensely selective critic of *GQ* magazine.

Vetri more than lived up to all the hype; it exceeded my expectations. I still can remember the two dishes that floored me: One was an asparagus flan with a suspended runny egg yolk in the center. It was light yet sultry and decadent. Then there was chestnut fettuccine with wild boar ragù and cocoa. I almost fell out of my chair, it was so good. Who was this Marc Vetri guy and what was this food I was eating? It certainly was way different from the meals I had cooked at the Italian Heritage Center! I asked for a job on the spot. Awaiting the answer was more nerve-racking than any date!

I jumped in headfirst, but it was a culture shock to say the least, and a true test. Up until that point, I had cooked only in high-volume restaurants that were all about the *mise en place*, where each dish was portioned out and prepared with expedience in mind. Vetri, on the other hand, was what we in the industry call *al momento*, with each and every dish made from scratch, start to finish. A turbot with potato torta? We would fillet the whole fish on the spot, peel the spuds then and there, and make the dish from beginning to end. Even the herbs were chopped to order. It was all so new to me and I just couldn't understand how to cook this way, but after about two months I started to get it together and somehow managed to survive this baptism by fire. Before long, I actually began to enjoy this new kamikaze style of cooking.

Instead of spending the first half of the day prepping and setting up stations, now I was baking bread, making petit fours and chocolates, and preparing a variety of *salumi*. Each and every day all the kitchen staff were wearing the hats of the baker, pastry chef, and salami maker. It was awesome.

I learned very early on that all cooking disciplines in the kitchen are equally important. You can't be a great sauté cook and not know how to butcher a fish. Whether it's cleaning vegetables, breaking down a pig, rolling dough, or mopping the floor, it is essential to be complete and consistent in every area. It is this understanding that has given me a less stereotypical approach to working with fresh flour. It has helped me view the craft of baking differently, too. Since I hadn't spent years tucked away in a restaurant pastry department, or doing the morning grind at a pâtisserie, my total ignorance of pastry allowed me to develop the majority of my skills in the kitchen and on the fly.

> My total ignorance of pastry allowed me to develop the majority of my skills in the kitchen.

After two years at Vetri, an identity crisis set in. I realized that my creativity and inspiration always came from what I ate at home and what I ate at restaurants. I knew how to cook, but I didn't know how to create something original. My chefs, Brad Spence and Jeff Michaud, were so successful and accomplished. What did I have to contribute? As much as I was learning from them, the idea of cooking Italian food without ever having been to Italy weighed on me. I needed to experience it for myself.

At this time I was reading a book called *Piano, Piano, Pieno: Authentic Food from a Tuscan Farm* by Susan McKenna Grant that detailed her life running an *agriturismo,* a working farm with tourist accommodations. The book was an inspiring collection of recipes that also described a sustainable life on her farm, where she reared animals, worked the land, and ran a guesthouse. To my surprise her email address was in the book, and I decided to reach out. I was amazed when within days she responded with an invitation to come work for her in Tuscany.

I told Marc of my intentions and offered as long a notice as he would need to fill my position at the restaurant. As his sous-chef, leaving wasn't something I took lightly. But, as any great mentor would do, he gave me great advice. He said as life-changing as working on Susan's farm in Italy might be, I would learn more as a chef if I cooked in a serious restaurant there instead. He told me he knew just the place. So at age twenty-six I was on my way to Bergamo, Italy, to work at Osteria della Brughiera. My time there was a revelation from the start. As any young Italian American cook might, I became fully intoxicated by the country itself. But more than that, I found myself learning daily lessons from professionals who were not only serious about their craft but also incredibly practiced and disciplined. These guys were carrying on traditions in the right way, the best way, and the way generations had been doing it before them. Everything they taught me—how to shape pasta, how to make a real panettone, even how to pull a perfect cappuccino—set a course for me that has been invaluable.

I loved Bergamo and had every intention of staying there. My Italian was getting good, and I loved the laid-back yet dynamic lifestyle. But then I got a call from Marc Vetri. He asked me if I was interested in coming back to Philly and taking a position as chef de cuisine. He was revamping the restaurant and wanted me to collaborate with him. It was an offer I couldn't refuse.

Before long I was back stateside, plotting and planning with Marc on how we could make Vetri even better. We wanted it to be not just a fine-dining place for Philadelphians, but rather the type of spot that would stand up nationally and hold its own with any Italian restaurant in New York and beyond. The first thing we decided was to turn Vetri from à la carte dining into a serious tasting-menu-only destination restaurant. With only thirty seats, we felt we had a real opportunity to make it a true culinary showcase. Mirroring Osteria della Brughiera, everything we did was handmade and we were committed to constant improvement.

Our hard work paid off. In 2012 Vetri was named a James Beard Foundation Award finalist for Outstanding Restaurant, *Travel + Leisure* named us among the Best Italian Restaurants in the United States, and I was named one of *Forbes* magazine's 30 Under 30 professionals in the food and wine industry. Now we were cooking! In spite of all these accolades, working at Vetri taught me never to rest on my laurels and I continued to learn as much as I could, especially through books. During my second year as chef de cuisine, I read *Cooking by Hand* by Paul Bertolli, the legendary California chef and Chez Panisse alum. I had been making pasta all along, but after reading his book, I couldn't get his words about milling grain out of my mind. I was haunted in the best way by romantic notions of Old World cooking. Eventually I went to Fante's, a hundred-year-old kitchen shop in South Philly's historic Italian Market, and bought a small mill for the restaurant. It scared me, mainly because it seemed like an ancient machine that might be too difficult to master. But I started experimenting, and before long I was milling flour every day.

> For the first time ever, I felt that the noodle could be—should be—the star of the show in a pasta dish.

From the very start I was amazed by the results. The fresh flour I was making for pasta was good enough to eat raw, and for the first time ever, I felt that the noodle could be—should be—the star of the show in a pasta dish, with the sauce playing the supporting role. As inspired as I was, I was terrified of transitioning the restaurant to freshly milled flour. I played the pitch over and over in my head: "Hey Marc, let's do only wacky pasta dishes and charge guests $150 for the tasting menu." It sounded just crazy enough for him to kill me. I didn't want to torpedo our successful new formula at the rejuvenated Vetri, which was enjoying a great reception. But I started gradually putting fresh-milled pastas on the menu, paying close attention to how guests responded.

At first it was just one: *pappardelle alfredo*, an egg yolk–rich noodle slathered in cream from Green Meadow Farm in Gap in Lancaster County, Pennsylvania, and dusted with Parmigiano-Reggiano from Hombre, the source for Massimo Bottura of Osteria Francescana in Modena and the Pope himself. It was a doubly safe and cautious move: everyone loves alfredo, so a cheeky riff with a wide noodle was hardly a reliable barometer. Nevertheless, it was a hit. Every plate came back clean and guests were actually commenting on the noodles themselves. Then I added ravioli with ricotta, lemon zest, and nutmeg. Our diners had the same reaction. I knew I was onto something.

Coincidentally, around the same time, Marc's friend chef Dan Barber emailed him an invitation to a seed conference he was hosting at Blue Hill Stone Barns that would feature forward-thinking discussions on wheat. The list of attendees was a who's who of top chefs from around the world, including Massimo Bottura and René Redzepi of Noma in Copenhagen. Marc went, of course, and he was blown away. Needless to say, after the conference he became a bit more interested in the flour experiments I had been doing. He couldn't stop telling me all he'd learned and he kept talking about this genius of a guy he'd met from Washington State University named Dr. Stephen Jones, the founder of the Bread Lab and one of the planet's foremost authorities on grains and flour. In spite of his academic focus, Dr. Jones made a major effort to reach out to chefs and kitchens across America to give his research a practical application. Within a week Marc was on a plane to the West Coast to visit him.

Over the next two years, Dr. Jones schooled us on wheat and flour at his Bread Lab at WSU. Not only did his work inspire our cooking in the restaurant, but it also gave us a much deeper understanding of the history of the grain and how it evolved from whole wheat to the white flour everyone uses today. It also opened up a vast network of mills and farmers that have been dedicated to fresh stone milling in reaction against the commodity flour industry. Soon my life was consumed with visits to mills all over the country. Some mills were right in our backyard. Just down the road in Bucks County, Fran and Mark Fischer's Castle Valley Mill supplied us with gorgeous stone-milled flour for bread and pasta. Farther away was Hayden Flour Mills in Arizona, which transformed my understanding of how pizza and pastry flour could behave.

> His work gave us a much deeper understanding of the history of the grain and how it evolved from whole wheat to the white flour everyone uses today.

One of the historical grains Dr. Jones worked with extensively was Red Russian wheat. With a distinctively bold flavor and a robust and resilient performance in the field, after years of testing it still yielded mediocre results when baked. As much as Dr. Jones and his team tried, the bread they produced was repeatedly unsatisfactory. His bakers had learned that when milled and mixed into a dough, Red Russian created a flabby mess. As all bakers know, the balance between elasticity and extensibility is key, and this stuff just wouldn't "bounce" back. You would stretch it while shaping and it would just remain all stretched out.

When Marc and I heard this, we thought, "Let's try making pasta with it!" We brought a bag of Red Russian back to Philly and got to work. The results were beautiful. We concluded that the gluten in the Red Russian wheat, although high in protein, was probably a weaker gluten and its structure was not strong enough to make bread. But for pasta it was perfect, most notably in its flavor. Even a plain noodle like fettuccine with no accompaniment was unbelievable. The high-protein flour also didn't require the amount of egg usually needed to get that "bite" you want from fresh pasta. For us, it was a groundbreaking revelation. Vetri was on its way to being the only Italian restaurant "bringing grain back" by using fresh flour across the whole menu.

After three years as chef de cuisine at Vetri, I felt it was time to move on and do my own thing. In 2015, I landed a dream job: to open a restaurant and manage all the food service in the Williamsburg Hotel in Brooklyn. The project started off with some pop-ups to test out menu items while the property was being built. This was fun initially, but I had come to New York to propel my career forward, not just to do pop-ups. The hotel still hadn't opened late that year. The owners were developing a city block into office spaces in Bushwick, a couple miles from the hotel. They asked me if I had any ideas for using part of it in the meantime. I pitched the Brooklyn Bread Lab, a space where I could continue to build on the milling techniques I had learned at Vetri, develop recipes for the hotel, and teach some classes on bread and pasta making. A month later, we were up and running.

I was giddy at the prospect of bringing milling back to Brooklyn. It had been decades since there was a functioning artisanal mill in the borough—eighty years, according to June Russell, head of the Greenmarket Regional Grains Project. I bought a stone mill that was by far the largest I had ever worked with; the pink granite stones weighed 500 pounds each and were driven by a 5-horsepower motor. For over a year, I used it to make flour for bread, pizza, pasta, and pastries. I was eager to open the hotel and feed all these wonderful freshly-milled-flour dishes to a wider audience. But after nearly two years of treading water in Brooklyn, the hotel had opened only one of its eight floors and the budget to finish the kitchen build-out was dried up. The gig wasn't going to pan out, so I took a job as the executive chef at Sessanta, in SoHo's SIXTY hotel.

In August 2017, five months into my tenure at Sessanta, my time there was cut short and my whole career trajectory was shaken up. A week later, I was on a plane to Germany and after a few months there, I was back in New York and plotting my next flour move, an opportunity I could hardly have imagined: my own restaurant (called Leonti!), on Manhattan's Upper West Side. The bread, pasta, and pastries are the product of years of contemplating the kind of creative modern Italian cuisine that makes New Yorkers feel nourished and nurtured. I hope you'll join me for a slice of bread, a forkful of pasta, or a sliver of cake.

HOW PROCESSING GRAIN HAS CHANGED

When I first started experimenting on a home mill at Vetri, I was immediately blown away by the results. The flavors of whatever I made were more intense, bolder, brighter, and just . . . better. It prompted questions that perplex me to this day: Why are we still using commodity flour from a supermarket or warehouse that was milled months or even years ago? Why do so many renowned and respected chefs, pastry chefs, bakers, and passionate home cooks choose to use it? Here's the hard truth: nearly all the baked goods we've been eating in the United States for the better part of a century and a half have been made with commodity flour. And until recently, there wasn't much choice for the average person. That is starting to change now—and I am hoping to do my part to promote a conversation about milling and grains. But how did we get here? It's tempting to think that the current state of grain is a recent occurrence and that if we could just go back to the way our grandparents ate, we could reclaim the flavors and nutrition of their youth. But our grandparents ate bad flour products, too. And so did their grandparents.

At the turn of the nineteenth century, wheat was planted mainly along the Eastern Seaboard, in the Southwest, and in Southern California. There were thousands of small mills across these regions—nearly 25,000 by the mid-eighteenth century—each milling diverse, locally cultivated wheats from the Old and New Worlds according to millennia-old stone-grinding technology. The flour produced by these mills was used to create nutrient-rich breads with exceptional flavor, but it couldn't travel very far due to the perishable nature of the wheat bran and germ.

Over the course of the early to mid-nineteenth century, grains and recipes migrated to America from Europe, along with new milling techniques. The roller-mill technology that initiated the industrial flour revolution was adapted in Hungary and introduced into the United States during this time. The roller mill was a modified version of a medieval Indian invention and its advent wasn't nefarious in and of itself. In fact, if the mechanism had been able to do its job without stripping out the nutrients, it would have been the greatest invention since sliced bread. After all, commodity milling produced more food for more people, and the flour's long shelf life meant it would be available whenever needed. Back then, the importance and nutritional value of vitamins, antioxidants, and fiber in grains was generally unknown.

With the rise of roller milling, white flour was marketed as more prestigious, and whole or darker flours were dismissed as too rustic and were relegated to the urban and rural poor. The commercial obsession with white flour was pervasive, but not without its skeptics. In the mid-nineteenth century, temperance advocate and minister Sylvester Graham preached a vegetarian diet—a radical concept at the time—based on home-milled whole grains. His eponymous invention, the Graham cracker, was a flavorful interruption to his otherwise bland diet. Possibly thanks to his strict diet, he died at age fifty-seven—a full twenty years beyond the average life span at the time—in 1851. Despite his small following, his teachings continued to resonate for a short time, but ultimately were overcome by large-scale farming. Soon the nation's thousands of small gristmills were shuttered as cheap commodity flour flowed by the ton from massive roller mills.

By the 1880s, industrial methods and their resulting commodity flour had solidified their total market domination, and grain stripped of its bran and germ (see page 34)—and therefore its nutrients—was the standard. This so-called white flour could be milled quickly and in huge quantities, and thanks to the absence of bran and germ it would not spoil, thereby creating a more commercially viable, shelf-stable product. The rise of railroads ensured that white flour could travel to every corner of the country and before long, unhealthy, flavorless flour was everywhere.

By the early twentieth century, large-scale farming and milling dominated the grain market and the number of commercial stone mills in the United States had dwindled to around two hundred. Americans were eating bread, pizza, pasta, and pastry made almost exclusively from commodity flour that was in the best cases nutrition-free and in the worst cases was pumped with chemicals to inhibit fungal growth.

Today the flour industry is, in a word, broken. But there is a silver lining in all this gloom: the number of small commercial stone mills and home millers is increasing. In spite of—or perhaps because of—commodity flour production, a growing number of millers, bakers, farmers, food safety advocates, and cooks are embracing a new way of growing and milling grains. The movements are numerous and diverse and scattered across the country; Maine, upstate New York, the Carolinas, the Pacific Northwest, Kansas, and Arizona are all home to thriving milling communities that are championing a small grain renaissance.

> A silver lining in all this gloom is that while we have an undoubtedly sick commodity flour market, small commercial stone mills and home millers are growing in number.

One of the nation's foremost authorities on wheat and wheat breeding is Dr. Stephen Jones, founder of Washington State University's Bread Lab. Since launching the program in 2010, Dr. Jones has trained students and farmers to grow and study different varieties of wheat, examine their properties, and assess how they would be useful to bakers, chefs, and home cooks. His decision to draw chefs into a conversation that was traditionally held by scientists was nothing short of revolutionary.

Meanwhile in New York, June Russell, head of the Greenmarket Regional Grains Project, built a phenomenal initiative that connects farmers and millers to chefs, bakers, and brewers. Such a network might seem unsurprising today, but getting it up and running was twenty years in the making; now, for the first time in some eighty years, city dwellers have access to a steady supply of local grains.

These ambassadors for the whole-grain movement have different motives, from reviving long-lost family traditions to promoting food sovereignty. What excites me about the movement is that there are so many points of view driving quality and innovation. And what motivates me to proselytize for whole grains is that I have seen that in order to keep the culture going, we have to be enthusiastic, vigilant, and a little loud. And I have no doubts that we are promoting a better way to farm, mill, and eat.

THE WILL TO MILL

Milling is the process of transforming grains into flour using—you guessed it—a mill. Here is a description of the various milling technologies, with suggestions on which mill will work best for you. With that information in mind, you can equip yourself with the tools you will need to start milling yourself.

TYPES OF MILLS

There are several different types of mills on the market—technically speaking, meat grinders, pepper grinders, and even your own teeth qualify—but not all of them are ideal for milling wheat for baking and cooking. Let's take a look at what's out there.

Stone Mills

Stone mills feature a circular bed stone, which is fixed to a platform. A runner stone of equal size spins on top of it, driven by animal, water, or electric power. As the runner stone turns, it cuts the grain into pieces, the size of which is determined by how close together or far apart the two stones are positioned. The resulting flour, consisting of milled bran, germ, and endosperm, is pushed into a series of tapered furrows and grooves that are cut into the stone. These act like a funnel to move the flour away from the mill and into a receptacle for collection. Although this is the most primitive form of milling, dating back to antiquity, stone-milling technology is the most reliable in terms of preserving the grain's nutritional integrity, as long as the mill doesn't heat up to more than 110°F through friction.

Hammer Mills

As the name suggests, the hammer mill works by repeatedly striking the grain. It was invented in China in the fourth century and was historically used in Europe's iron workshops until it was adapted for food production. Its metal pieces bang on grain and other products to break them into small fragments. It is especially adapted to transforming corn or wheat into animal feed, which is indeed a major destination for American grains. It could hypothetically be used to transform grains into a fine powder, which would be great for cakes, but I wouldn't recommend it.

Roller Mills

The roller mill first appeared on the Indian subcontinent in the Middle Ages and was used mainly for grinding sugar and processing cotton. In the nineteenth century, the roller method was adapted in Europe and the United States for milling wheat. These mills consist of two or more cylinders, somewhat resembling large ribbed rigatoni, that spin in opposite directions at different speeds, stripping away the bran and germ, leaving the crushed endosperm (in other words, white flour) in their wake. The mill works quickly and gained popularity for its efficiency and ability to create a nonperishable product (aided by the absence of bran and germ, the flour is practically inert).

Roller mills are favored by industry, and the vast majority of the commodity flour on the market is ground in one. They produce a shelf-stable white flour that has been stripped of its flavor, character, and nutrients. Roller mills aren't available for home use and even if they were, I wouldn't want to use the flavorless flour they produce.

Burr Mills

You probably already have a burr mill in your kitchen cabinet. Most pepper mills and many coffee grinders work on the burr system, in which interwoven metal teeth crush the product. The process generates some heat and is not the most efficient way to mill large quantities of flour, but my buddy the documentary filmmaker and flour enthusiast JD McLelland uses a burr mill outfitted with a custom cooling system, which helps him maintain the integrity of the wheat as he mills. Unfortunately, this homemade rigging isn't for sale. I stick to a burr mill for making rice flour (see page 74) and never use one for milling wheat.

BUYING A MILL

When it comes to buying a mill, stick to stone. You have a few options depending on your needs, space constraints, and budget. Whether you're a professional or a beginner, the Mockmill attachment to KitchenAid, Kenmore, AEG, and Electrolux mixers is a great option and one of the most affordable, costing around $200. It can mill grains as well as corn, legumes, and coffee—most things that a full-scale mill does—but it's more efficient for smaller amounts. I have found that, in spite of factory specifications, which report on the conservative side, you can mill up to 10 pounds of flour in an hour. You can use the Mockmill for any recipe in this book. Thanks to the portability of a stand mixer, you can move it around more easily than the heavier mills described below. The Mockmill 100 and 200 models sit on your countertop and are good for milling small amounts of flour, though they generate a great deal of heat when the motor runs for a long time. The Mockmill Professional 100 and 200 models have specialty self-cooling motors designed to run nonstop.

For a step up in price and a more nostalgic design, the KoMo Magic Grain Mill starts at $439 for a 3-inch millstone sheathed in beechwood. It can be used for milling grains, legumes, and coffee. The KoMo mill sits on the tabletop and is about the same size as a blender, so it can be stored in a cabinet. It works off a small motor and can mill about 18 pounds of flour in an hour.

For professional kitchens, I recommend the Meadows 8-inch mill. You can choose between a 1- and a 2-horsepower motor. If you're milling mostly soft wheat, go for the 1-horsepower motor. If you are planning to mill mainly hard wheat, get the 2-horsepower motor. Naturally, if you're working with a mix of the two, choose the more powerful motor. This mill can produce 50 pounds of flour in an hour, which is more than most restaurants need, but it would be great for a bakery or a pizzeria. The mill's full dimensions vary according to the model. I like the model measuring 32 × 34 × 57 inches, which also has a stand for a flour bag. The millstone weighs 250 pounds, so it's not easy to move around; keep that in mind when positioning it in your work space. It retails from $2,500.

Although all these mills can grind legumes and rice, I often mill these separately in a burr mill or another type of coffee-grinding equipment. You'll need to mill dried fava beans into flour for the Sourdough Durum Loaf (page 94) and rice into flour for dusting that loaf as well as the Yeasted Loaf (page 71) and for making the Shortbread Cookies (page 224) and the Rice Flour Mixture (page 74).

MILL MAINTENANCE

If possible, avoid running your mill without feeding grain into it. The very first time you use your mill, mill about 5 pounds of cheap wheat berries and discard the flour. This will clean out any stone dust. To begin milling for edible flour production, turn the mill on and calibrate the machine according to the manufacturer's instructions. Turn the dial to draw the stones together until they barely touch, then gently back them off. Turn the machine off until it has cooled down completely. Turn the mill back on. Working with 1 cup of grain at a time, test the mill for the desired fineness; then adjust the stones until your flour reaches the coarseness or fineness you are looking for.

When you mill soft wheat as opposed to hard wheat (see page 39), you can pull the stones farther apart and still get the fineness you want for your flour, allowing you to run the mill at a faster speed while reducing the heat created through friction. Less heat preserves the integrity of the grain while reducing the risk of the mill sparking and starting a fire.

A beautiful thing about millstones is that they are made of a durable material, and with a little maintenance, they can last for a long time—even centuries. Maintenance is basic. Before and after milling, dust the stones with a clean, dry kitchen towel. Never use soap or water to clean the mill. Store your mill in a dry place.

CUSTOMIZING FLOUR

Bran is a key source of flavor and fiber in pasta and baked goods, but its structure—it behaves somewhat like a sharp blade when mixed into dough—can disrupt gluten development. For that reason, many recipes in this book feature extracted, or sifted, flour. Chapter openers will let you know the amount of bran to use—this will be stated as a percentage of bran inclusion. And ingredients lists for individual recipes will indicate where this percentage varies from the initial chapter instructions.

A flour with 100% inclusion is a whole wheat flour, while a flour with 30% inclusion has had 70% of its bran sifted out, or extracted. To sift the bran out of the flour, you'll need a #70 mesh sieve, which costs about $100 at specialty retailers, but you can substitute a pollen sifter, available online for closer to $35. When milling extracted flour at home, sift out the bran using the sieve, then reintroduce the recommended percentage of bran by weight back into the flour.

HEAT

Stone-milled flour is produced through friction, which generates heat. The finer the flour, the more heat is generated through friction. If I am milling superfine flour, I will pass wheat berries through the mill twice—the first time on a very coarse setting and the second time on a finer setting. Whatever the fineness of the flour I am aiming for, I always mill wheat berries straight out of the fridge. Constantly monitor the temperature of the flour with a probe thermometer, taking care to keep it below 110°F. If you see the temperature climb, back up the stones and mill more coarsely.

SAFETY

Always refer to the mill manufacturer's instructions before getting started. When milling, avoid wearing a tie, necklace, or any garment that could get caught in the machine. Pull back long hair. Never leave the mill running unattended.

WORDS TO KNOW

AUTOLYZE: A pre-hydration period in which flour and water are mixed together and allowed to rest before any other ingredients get involved. This one-on-one time hydrates the flour thoroughly and activates the enzymes that help with the bread-making process. It also allows you to do less mixing when you add the other ingredients.

CRUMB: A bread's internal structure. It can be airy and open, dense and closed, or somewhere in between. Crumb is affected by a number of factors, including the flour's strength, the length of time a dough ferments, and the amount of water in the dough.

EXTENSIBILITY: The degree to which a dough can be stretched without breaking. Certain flours (such as Sonora and Red Russian) have good extensibility.

EXTRACTION: Passing flour through a sieve to remove the bran; also known as "sifting."

INCLUSION: The percentage of bran by weight in flour.

LAMINATING: The process of folding and rolling butter into dough to create a pastry featuring dough layers separated by strata of butter. Whole Wheat Croissants (page 221) and Puff Pastry (page 211) are the ultimate examples of this type of pastry.

LEVAIN: A sourdough starter made by mixing flour and water and allowing them to ferment naturally as yeasts and bacteria in the environment and in the freshly milled wheat seed itself "infect" the mixture. Levain may be used on its own for fermenting doughs or in combination with commercial yeast.

SEMOLINA: A coarse grind of durum wheat that is often used for dusting peels or kitchen towels used to wrap pasta dough.

STARCH QUALITY: The ability of the starch in a flour to absorb water without breaking down. Good starch quality signifies a flour that keeps its integrity in a high-hydration dough.

WHEAT BERRIES: Cleaned and dried whole kernels that can be milled into flour.

ALL ABOUT WHEAT

Without being hyperbolic I can confidently say that wheat is one of the most important foods on Earth. Virtually every civilization relies on wheat in some form for nutrition and calories.

WHAT'S WHEAT?

Wheat is a grain that was domesticated in the Fertile Crescent, a fecund area in the Middle East, more than 10,000 years ago. Over the past ten millennia, wheat has moved from the banks of the Tigris and Euphrates rivers to every continent but Antarctica. It is among the most widely grown foods in the world. Today it ranks third among US agricultural products, behind corn and soybeans.

THE LIFE OF WHEAT

The size and shape of the grains may vary, but all wheat berries are made up of the same basic components: bran, germ, and endosperm. The bran is the fibrous shell that encases the seed, accounting for about 14% of the seed's total weight. Bran transmits a tremendous amount of flavor and is a source of fiber, which aids in digestion. The germ, essentially the seed's embryo, accounts for 2.5% of the grain's weight. The remaining weight is endosperm, a component rich in protein and carbohydrates but rather lacking in flavor. Unsifted flour is whole wheat, while extracted flour has been sifted to eliminate the bran and germ. It is pure endosperm, or white flour.

The wheat plant is formed of a stalk, which in turn grows seeds. In order to thrive, wheat requires only water, sunshine, and soil, so it has adapted to numerous climates—though certain wheats do better in particular environments or perform differently in disparate climates (see page 40). As it grows and matures, the wheat kernel turns from green to beige, golden, reddish, or even purple-tinged. When the wheat is ready to be harvested, farmers cut the grain down—in the past they would use a scythe but today they use a machine called a combine—and then process it. Depending on the scale of the farming facility, a farmer may clean, separate, and dry the seed or entrust these steps to a miller. In either case, the next stage is extracting the seeds from the chaff, a scaly protective casing also known as the hull.

The hull is removed through a tumbling process that gently massages it off the seed while airflow blows it away, separating the hull from the grain. After the hull is removed and discarded, the grain is inspected once again and separated from field debris (such as other seeds) using either a series of perforated plates that separate items of unlike sizes or pneumatic air chambers. Next, the grain is dried with currents of warm or hot air, ideally over hours or even days. Controlling the temperature is key to keeping the grain healthy: any temperature over 110°F damages the seed's internal structure. Industrial drying units can reach 180°F; big roller-mill plants (see page 27) don't need to preserve

the seed's energy and structure because the entire industrial flour industry relies on the long shelf life of essentially dead flour. Stone mills (see page 27), on the other hand, capture all the nutritious parts of the grain, and the nutrition of the resulting flour is preserved if it is dried in low-temperature drying chambers. Because wheat kernels are live seeds, the drying process is an important step for preserving them; a properly dried kernel can be shelf stable for years. When the seed is dried to a 12% to 15% moisture content, it is resistant to rancidity and sprouting and can be milled for human or animal consumption when the time comes.

WHEAT STATS

No two grain harvests are identical. Some farms and mills provide the following key specs on their packaging or websites, or can furnish them upon request, allowing you to track these variables and use them to modify recipes as needed. Here are some of the figures you might encounter:

Protein Count

The amount of protein present in wheat species ranges from 8% to 17%; the overall protein content depends on both the genetics of the individual grain species and the conditions in which the grain has grown. A flour from a Sonora soft wheat grown in California may have a slightly different protein content than one from a Sonora grown in Arizona. Similarly, if you grow emmer in a dry climate, it has a greater net protein content than grain from the very same seeds grown in a wet climate, as rain "washes away" protein. While rainfall, climate, and farming techniques all influence the final characteristics of the wheat, there are some baselines. For example, durum's protein content may vary, but it rarely drops below 12%, regardless of where or how it grows.

Gluten protein accounts for 75% to 85% of a wheat's total protein content. When gluten protein comes into contact with water, two compounds are activated: glutenins and gliadins, which give the milled wheat elasticity and extensibility, respectively. The ratio of glutenins to gliadins influences the gluten strength, making certain flours better adapted to either rising or stretching—or both or neither. Common practice calls for a protein content of 11.5% to 14% in flour for bread baking. But by using baking techniques like higher hydration, levain, and cold fermentation, you can achieve a similar product with a flour with lower protein without sacrificing structure or flavor. Managing a grain's characteristics is essential to freestyle baking, but the recipes in this book address the basics for choosing the best one for the job.

Falling Number

The falling number of a wheat, also known as the Hagberg Number, was developed as a way of analyzing how its resulting flour would perform. The definition of this internationally standardized figure, which is measured on a scale of zero to 500, is especially useful for guessing a flour's potential enzymatic activity. For example, a low Hagberg Number signifies reduced milling quality.

Since fresh grains are viable seeds, they are filled with enzymes that provide the energy to make a planted seed grow. When a seed is instead milled into flour, mixed with water and yeast, and fermented, the enzymes in the seed become fuel for the yeast and propel the fermentation process. The resulting dough captures the product of that energy transition in its gluten network. This energy can be quantified with lab tests; the lower the number, the more enzymatic activity present in the grain.

A plant contains a lot of enzymatic activity as it's growing. Generally speaking, a grain harvested and milled young will have lots of activity and a lower falling number, while an older harvest will result in a higher number on the scale. There are some exceptions, however. An older harvest that experienced certain environmental triggers like high humidity, excessive rainfall, or "cold shock" brought on by frost can exhibit a low falling number. Whether shopping for whole grains or milled flour, look for products with a falling number around 250, which is ideal for fermenting doughs. A falling number above 350, generally speaking, needs help to ferment since it is not as active; bakers often add sugar or malt syrup or another fuel to compensate for the lack of enzymatic activity. Anything under 200 is considered very active, difficult to tame, and apt to cause a dough to overferment.

A falling number outside the ideal range does not necessarily signal that the grain was unhealthy when it was harvested; instead it could indicate that it was not harvested at the ideal time. Sometimes farmers have to harvest early or late to accommodate weather events, leading to less-than-optimal falling number statistics. Some farms and mills furnish this figure on their packaging or websites or upon request after scientific testing.

To ascertain the falling number, a lab will make a slurry with flour and water, drop it into a test tube, and time how long it takes to break down. When I get a shipment of flour, I do my own version of this test, making a little dumpling with flour and water. I drop it in water and time how long it takes to break down. The quicker it dissolves, the more active the sample. Another test I do is to make a simple dough from flour and water, set it aside, and check it throughout the day, pulling and stretching it to see how it behaves as it ages. This primitive test will give me an idea of whether the enzymatic activity is slow, medium, or fast; if the dough holds together, the activity is slow or medium, whereas if it falls apart, the activity is fast. Neither experiment is as precise as a lab analysis, of course, but it gives me an idea of how active the flour is. Based on the guesstimated activity, I can adjust the amount of yeast or sourdough starter I add to a dough.

Water Absorption
The percentage of a flour's weight that it can absorb in water is measured with a farinograph, a tool that analyzes the amount of water a flour's starch can hold before it becomes saturated and indicates how long a dough can be hydrated before it breaks down. This is particularly important for working with durum wheats, which generally deteriorate more rapidly than other wheats if they are too hydrated.

Some farms and mills provide water absorption statistics, but most small operations, including the majority of the mills listed in the Resources section (page 247), don't have the instruments to do so. To determine it in my own semi-scientific way, I mix flour and water together and monitor how the slurry deteriorates over the course of a day.

The presence or absence of bran affects water absorption; bran is thirsty and sucks up a lot of water, so a whole wheat flour with 100% bran inclusion (see page 30) will take up to 10% more water than a sifted flour of the same grain variety.

WHEAT VARIETIES

Around 30,000 varieties of wheat exist, but relatively few are grown commercially. Wheat falls into two broad families: *Triticum aestivum,* common wheat, which accounts for around 95% of global production, and *Triticum durum*, durum wheat. In the United States, farmers categorize wheats based on color, growing season, and hardness. The permutations created by these overlapping categories are dizzying, so I have tried to simplify the topic as much as possible, focusing only on the types of wheat used in this book.

Red Versus White

The kernels of red wheats have a reddish hue from pigment found mainly in the bran, while white wheats are golden or cream colored. Most wheats are either white or red. There are some exceptions, such as Blue Beard durum, which has a purplish color, and rye, which is silvery. The colors used to describe wheat are simply descriptors and are not related to quality or flavor.

Winter Versus Spring

Winter wheats are planted in the fall and sprout 4 to 6 inches before falling into a hibernation period of sorts called vernalization, when the temperature falls below 40°F or 50°F. The plants aren't actually slumbering, but rather undergoing a series of internal reactions that will facilitate their growth come spring. As soon as the soil warms, the plants become active again and grow until they mature and are harvested in the summer. Spring wheats are planted when the ground thaws in the spring and they typically mature faster than winter wheats. They are also harvested in the summer. Because winter wheats have an extended growing season, they deplete more of their nutrients and therefore generally have lower protein (10% to 12% on average) than spring wheats (12% to 14% on average). The higher protein content of spring wheats generally translates into greater gluten potential, which allows you to make breads or pizza doughs that ferment for a long time and can trap lots of air.

Hard Versus Soft

Grain hardness is just that. Hard wheats are more difficult to mill than soft wheats; their components are more densely packed into the endosperm cells. Hard wheats have high protein and gluten potential, which makes them ideal for yeasted breads that must trap carbon dioxide in their gluten network. They can be used for a wide range of baked goods, too. Soft wheats, on the other hand, contain a high proportion of carbohydrate and relatively low gluten potential, making them a good choice for more delicate baked items like pastry and cakes.

WHEAT SPECIES   Each variety of wheat has its own advantages. One isn't better than another, although certain wheats work better for certain recipes, either on their own or as a blend. There is also variation in the same grain grown in different climates, as well as variation in the same crop from one year to the next. Hard winter wheat that grows in New Jersey isn't going to have a high protein content when compared with the same wheat grown in the Arizona desert, but it may end up having the same protein content as a Kansas Turkey wheat grown in—you guessed it—Kansas. Getting to know the characteristics and potential of each grain will help you understand my flour choices in each recipe and eventually help you to make your own choices.

Ancient Grains

Over the past decade or so, ancient grains, so called because they were domesticated thousands of years ago, have surged in popularity. Many such grains are low-yield, low-demand, and quite expensive. Therefore they require a concerted effort on the part of farmers, bakers, millers, and consumers to help them survive in the marketplace. This has driven marketing campaigns that suggest they are superior to all other grains.

There is an objective benefit to eating ancient grains. In fact, they are easier to process than modern grain varietals thanks to their low molecular weight. Additionally, they offer great flavor because they haven't had taste inadvertently bred out of them in favor of performance and yield, as many modern grains have.

EINKORN (*TRITICUM MONOCOCCUM*) has a high protein content but is low in gluten potential. There are only a handful of einkorn producers in the United States, and at a wholesale cost of around $3.50 a pound the grain is more expensive than pork! I have a tough time making bread with it on its own, so I like mixing it with other flours. Commercially, einkorn is also labeled "enkir" or "farro piccolo."

SPELT (*TRITICUM SPELTA*) is high in protein—averaging around 13% to 14%, it's about the same as durum—but low in gluten. It has a subtly sweet and nutty flavor, and indeed, bakers and chefs use it as much for its taste as they do for its protein. Commercially, spelt is sometimes called "farro grande."

RYE (*SECALE CEREALE*) is categorized by some farmers, bakers, and institutions as wheat, while others draw a distinction. As its binomial nomenclature suggests, it is not part of the *Triticum* genus, but it is a close relative of wheat, and it is an ancient grain that

originated in central Anatolia in the Iron Age. It has a sweet, nutty flavor that shines through whether you ferment it to bake bread or use it unfermented in pasta or cookie dough. The fiber-rich cereal is low in gluten potential and for centuries has been the cornerstone of Central and Eastern European and Scandinavian baking traditions, so for our purposes I have included it here.

Hard Winter Wheat

Some recipes in this book simply list "hard winter wheat flour" as an ingredient, but I always list my preferred flour alongside. In these cases, you can use the suggested wheat or any other from this category. When shops, farms, and mills are selling a well-known wheat variety like the ones mentioned below, sometimes they explicitly state the variety on the label, and sometimes they simply label the package generically as "Hard Winter Wheat," without referring to a specific type. Some companies prefer to keep things simple for customers who might otherwise be wary of unfamiliar wheat varieties. Although the marketplace is changing, perceived consumer response still guides grain and flour labeling.

EDISON HARD WINTER WHEAT is a collaborative breeding effort from autodidact wheat breeder Merrill Lewis and WSU's Bread Lab. It grows mainly in the Pacific Northwest and the Northeast and imparts delicate, buttery flavors. I recommend it for pizza doughs.

Hard Red Winter Wheat

Grown in the High Plains, especially in Kansas, hard red winter wheat is high in protein and strong in gluten potential. It's great for buns, rolls, and yeasted loaves. Several types are used in the recipes in this book.

WARTHOG HARD RED WINTER WHEAT averages around 11% protein and has an intense wheat flavor. It's an all-around solid performer, bringing strength, good starch quality, and extensibility to doughs. I recommend it for yeasted and sourdough breads.

RED FIFE HARD RED WINTER WHEAT is named for its reddish color and for the Canadian farmer, Dave Fife, who commercialized it. Red Fife is known for its warm, nutty, sweet flavor. Although its exact origins are unknown, it likely came from Eastern Europe. It was introduced to Canada via the Fife farm in the 1840s. This all-around performer is good for pasta, bread, cookies, and cakes.

REDEEMER HARD RED WINTER WHEAT averages around 13% protein, has a mild flavor, and is stronger and absorbs more water than Warthog. It's one of my favorite bread flours.

KANSAS TURKEY WHEAT was introduced to Kansas by Mennonites in 1874. I reach for this grain for its high protein and starch quality. Its flavor isn't quite as remarkable as that of Red Fife. I use it for pasta and pizza doughs or in blends for pastry.

Soft White Wheat

This genre of wheats has a naturally white color and is perfect for delicate doughs, especially when it is finely milled. Frederick and Sonora are the soft white wheats that appear in this book. Some recipes simply list "soft white wheat flour" as an ingredient, but I always list my preferred flour alongside. In these cases, you can use the suggested wheat or any other from this category.

FREDERICK SOFT WHITE WHEAT makes a silky, white, and fluffy flour. It has low gluten potential and is ideal for flaky pastries.

SONORA SOFT WHITE WHEAT was first isolated in the mountain plains of Sonora, Mexico, in the early 1700s. Sonora thrives in arid desert climates like its native Mexico, Arizona, and California. It is very extensible, inexpensive, and absorbent, and has a subtle wheat flavor that's never overwhelming. Low in both protein and gluten, it's ideal for soft pastries and for blending with harder wheats that lack flavor or extensibility.

GLUTEN ISN'T EVIL

The grain market—like that of all industries—is shaped by trends and influenced by marketing. This weakness has been laid bare by the anti-gluten movement. Gluten is a protein that is produced when flour is mixed with water. It occurs in almost all grain-based bread, pizza, pasta, and pastry, although there are a small number of grains that don't have any gluten potential at all, such as teff and buckwheat. Gluten itself is not naturally present in flour, but is activated by adding water, which creates the protein network.

Over the past decade, gluten has been demonized by the health food and diet industries. This anti-gluten movement is *not* related to the very serious celiac disease, an autoimmune illness present in around 1% of the population. People with celiac disease cannot consume gluten without serious adverse health effects. Yet more than one in three Americans has "taken a break" from gluten because of either a diagnosed or a perceived intolerance, neither of which is specifically the result of gluten itself but of reactions to commodity flour. Industrial flour is rife with compounds that could affect digestion and health. Meanwhile, the absence of bran and germ, the very substances that aid digestion and make flour "whole," can turn the flour into an allergen of sorts.

Both scientific and anecdotal sources report that individuals with "gluten intolerance" can consume products made with whole grains, supporting the theory that gluten isn't, in fact, evil. Commodity flour, on the other hand, may very well be.

Durum Wheat

Durum means "hard" in Latin, and durum wheats (*Triticum durum*) are related to historic grains like spelt (see page 40). They have high gluten potential and generally are amber in color; purple-tinged Blue Beard is an exception. Durum is often used for pasta—its hardness contributes to an al dente texture. Durum gluten lacks elasticity, so the flour benefits from blending when making certain pasta shapes like orecchiette and cavatelli (page 147). It breaks down quickly, so I avoid using it in high-hydration doughs such as ciabatta (page 77). Blue Beard and Iraq durum are the two durum varieties used in this book's recipes.

BLUE BEARD DURUM WHEAT (*TRITICUM TURGIDUM*), native to Iran, is named for the hue of its husk, which turns purplish-blue as it matures. It's high in protein and low in gluten and has wonderful tropical fruit flavors, including banana. Blue Beard is ideal for slow-fermented breads, rustic baking, and pastas.

IRAQ DURUM WHEAT (*TRITICUM TURGIDUM*), originally from Iraq, was revived by Monica Spiller, founder of the Whole Grain Connection, a nonprofit organization that promotes whole grains. It is prized for the golden color and subtle sweetness it imparts to breads and pastas.

BUYING FRESHLY MILLED FLOUR AND WHEAT BERRIES FOR HOME MILLING

The recipes in this book were developed with and are meant to be made with freshly milled flour. The ideal is to use flour that has been milled immediately before you start in on a recipe. Obviously, this is easiest to do if you are milling at home, but you can also purchase freshly milled flour from millers (see page 247), specialty shops, supermarkets, and farmers' markets. You can purchase wheat berries for milling from the same sources.

For the best product, look for flour or wheat berries that are fresh and are the product of organic (or biodynamic) agriculture. But before you jump into buying anything, read up on wheat species (page 40), understand the characteristics of each, then make your choices based on what you plan to cook—or choose what you want to cook based on the abilities of the wheat.

Buying Flour from a Mill

The mills I recommend are reputable, but if you purchase milled flour via mail order, you lose control over the temperature of the flour while it is in transit, which may accelerate its deterioration. Always refrigerate or freeze freshly milled flour—or at least keep it in a cool, dry place—in a sealed container.

Each miller will have their own specifications for how their operation runs. Some sell their own flour blends that they have developed for pastry, pizza, pasta, and bread, while others focus on varietal flours milled from specific wheats. Both the blends and the

varietal flours are milled with the end use in mind. Flour for pastries is generally milled very fine, while you will encounter a whole range of coarseness for bread. The coarseness of the flour is sometimes indicated as "00" or "semolina"; both references come from Italian milling, but the United States lacks a defined system, so consult your miller for their precise specifications.

If you're lucky enough to have an artisanal stone mill near you, the flour won't have to travel very far, which is ideal for maintaining its integrity. When I buy flour from a miller, I always ask these questions:

- *Where does the grain come from?* For me, local is best.
- *How was it grown?* I recommend flour milled from wheat that was the product of organic or biodynamic agriculture.
- *Who grew it?* I want grain that was grown on a small farm by people who are paid a fair wage.
- *How was the grain cleaned?* As simply as possible, I hope.
- *How was it stored?* A cool, dry place is the only acceptable answer.
- *How finely was the flour milled?* I use this information to determine what recipe it might work for, and, based on the cues in this book, you can do the same.

Be sure to note the "milled on" date—most flours begin deteriorating two weeks after milling and retain their nutritional value and peak flavor only for that period. However, many vendors print a "use by" date extended up to two months. To maximize freshness and limit waste, order only the quantity of flour that you need.

Buying Wheat Berries from Farmers or Millers

Farmers, like chefs, are trying to run a tough, low-margin business. There are amazing farmers out there, but even some of my favorite farms with whom I have had long-established relationships have tried to unload a little second-rate stuff on me now and again. The same goes for millers, who often sell wheat berries in addition to freshly milled flour.

To be sure you are getting the best wheat berries possible, ask questions like those above in addition to:

- *How was the grain dried?* I make the purchase only if the response is "slowly and at a low temperature."
- *When was the grain harvested?* I want a product that was harvested within a year at the most.
- *Do you know any bakers who have worked with these grains? What kinds of recipes have they had success with?* I often get inspired by how others have used the grains I'm buying.

- *Was the wheat tested for bacteria and fungus?* Hopefully it was and came back clean! I always check to see if any of the wheat is pink—if so, then it is infected with an undesirable fungus. Smell and taste the grain. It should have a wheaty aroma and taste good. If it smells like cinnamon, that signals a fungus problem. And if it tastes bad, it probably won't make very delicious bread, pizza, pasta, or pastry.

Buying Flour and Wheat Berries from a Supermarket

On supermarket shelves you will find packages that are labeled simply "Hard Winter Wheat Flour" or "Wheat Berries." In these cases, you won't be able to precisely predict the product's characteristics or capacities and you will have to use trial and error to test its strengths and weaknesses.

In regions of the United States where there are robust grain cultures and vibrant milling movements, the stores are more advanced when it comes to labeling, the variety of grains offered, and the attention to provenance. Upstate New York is at the helm, and Wegmans supermarket chain has even built a mill in its Rochester flagship. Whole Foods locations across the Northeast source flour from small stone mills, but the bags can be twice as expensive as purchasing directly from the mill of origin. Organic whole food stores typically sell a range of wheat berries and stone-milled flours, though labeling specificity varies.

KEEPING WHEAT BERRIES AND FLOUR FRESH

Properly dried wheat berries are shelf stable and keep well in an airtight container in a cool, dry place for years. Freshly milled flour, on the other hand, is much more perishable. As soon as the grain is milled, its interior structure is exposed to oxygen and begins to deteriorate. Keep flour in a sealed container, ideally in your refrigerator or freezer. Label your flour with the "milled on" date and, if possible, use it within two weeks of milling.

COOKING
WITH
FRESH
FLOUR

HOW TO USE THESE RECIPES

The recipes in this book are divided into four chapters: bread, pasta, pizza, and pastry. Each chapter starts with an explanation of how to choose the right grain for a recipe, how to mill and sift flour, and other details that will help you use the recipes that follow and take away what you learn in order to embrace freshly milled flour as a regular part of your cooking. Many of the recipes provide tips for customizing, either with alternative flour choices or with additional ingredients for a different flavor. At the end of the pasta and pizza chapters, I include recipes for sauces and toppings, respectively. You'll notice that some recipes are intentionally spread across multiple pages so that the steps appear adjacent to their matching photo to help you get the most out of this book.

COOKING TIPS

Always read the entire recipe before beginning to cook. Some recipes require time-sensitive prep work, which will be mentioned in the headnote. A number of recipes include levain (page 90) or *biga* (page 102), which must be prepared in advance; other recipes have long fermentation periods that you must take into account.

I have written the recipes with metric measurements for ingredients and US units for standard baking trays and dishes. I strongly urge you to use a digital metric scale in order to achieve the most successful results.

Most of the bread and pizza doughs should be mixed in a stand mixer, but shaping is done by hand. This puts you in direct contact with the dough and forges a bond between you and the final product. Handling the dough will also give you a greater understanding of how flour and water react, what happens to the dough as it ferments, how strong it is, and when it is perfectly risen. Learn the basic methods I recommend and feel free to make small changes in your cooking as necessary to accommodate any differences in the type of flour you are using.

In addition to these suggestions, I urge you to commit your most precious resource: time. Practice your craft. Your favorite bakers didn't become who they are by chance; they focused on honing their skills and committed themselves to revisiting and improving recipes and techniques.

EQUIPMENT

If you bought this book, you are already on your way to making better bread, pasta, pizza, and pastry, but there are a few cooking implements that will be helpful as you get started. Odds are, you already have some of them in your kitchen. A handful of recipes call for special equipment—a banneton for proofing yeasted and sourdough loaves, for example—but most can be adapted to items you already have. When possible I have provided alternatives for special equipment.

DIGITAL SCALE

Before you even start thinking about milling at home, get the tool that will give you the most consistent results. If you are not willing to invest in this very affordable and essential item, this project isn't going to work. A scale will give you a precision baseline to build on. Ideally, you want a scale that displays at least one digit to the right of the decimal point. If your grandma, like mine, never measured anything, remember that she had decades of experience. Using a scale will help you get there faster. Metric measurements are more precise, which is why you'll notice that I haven't included US measurements unless the quantity doesn't need to be precise.

For making bread, pizza, and pastries, weighing ingredients is a crucial step to success. Baking, after all, is an exact science. Cup measures can vary significantly and different flours have slightly differing weights per cup, so using a digital scale is the only foolproof method for ensuring you'll achieve the intended results. For pasta making, precise measurements are slightly less crucial.

BOWLS

You'll need small, medium, and large bowls, preferably glass, stainless steel, or plastic, for mixing doughs, levain, and *biga*.

BAKING SHEETS

Baking sheets come in different sizes, the most versatile being a rimmed half-sheet (13 × 18 inches). These recipes were developed and tested with half-sheets, but in most cases, any size should work fine.

PARCHMENT PAPER

You'll need parchment paper to line springform pans, roll out pie dough and butter blocks, line baking sheets, and transfer dough onto a preheated surface in the oven.

SIEVE

A mesh sieve is essential for sifting flour. I use a #70 mesh to extract my flour.

POTS AND PANS

The recipes in this book that call for specific baking vessels were tested using the following equipment:

- a standard 6-quart Dutch oven
- a 13 × 4 × 4-inch Pullman loaf pan with a cover
- 8-inch springform pans
- 9-inch round cake pans
- 12-inch fluted tart pans and springform pans
- muffin tins

BENCH SCRAPER

A bench scraper (also known as a dough scraper) is useful for handling and transferring dough. Think of it as a nonstick extension of your own hands. It also works wonders for cleaning your work surface, dividing dough into pieces, and cutting ingredients together, as in the case of Potato Gnocchi (page 150). It's also a handy tool for scraping up excess flour from the work surface, which I recommend you collect in a container to use as bench flour (see the tip on page 138).

MIXERS

Most of the bread and pizza recipes require a stand mixer fitted with a dough hook attachment, while many of the pastry recipes employ the paddle. A KitchenAid or similar mixer can be fitted with the Mockmill attachment (see page 29) for milling fresh flour.

BAKING STONES, PEELS, AND RACKS

For evenly baked bread and pizza, use a baking stone. Inverted baking sheets or unglazed quarry tiles make good substitutes. In all cases, you'll want to preheat the stone, baking sheet, or tiles in the oven at the recommended baking temperature for at least 45 minutes before you bake. Doing so ensures that you will transfer the dough to the ideal surface for even cooking.

A peel is used to smoothly transfer bread or pizza dough to and from the baking surface in the oven. You can improvise a peel with a flat, thin wooden board or a rimless baking sheet; even a piece of cardboard or plywood, or a basic metal sheet will do.

To ensure your final product doesn't get damp and steamy after baking, set it aside on a cooling rack until cooled.

SHAPING LINEN AND PROOFING BASKETS

A *couche* is a stiff baking linen that is used to shape baguettes and other loaves during their final proofing phase. To prepare the *couche*, fold the linen lengthwise to form two valleys. Dust the valleys liberally with a rice flour mixture (see page 74), bench flour (see the tip on page 138), or bran, then fit the shaped dough into the valleys to proof. Baguettes (page 97) go through their final proofing in an 18 × 24-inch *couche*.

Use a banneton, or proofing basket, to help loaves hold their shape as they ferment. The Yeasted Loaf (page 71) is proofed in a 2-kilogram basket. The Sourdough Loaf (page 81) and Sourdough Durum Loaf (page 94) are proofed in two 1-kilogram bannetons.

A *couche* and bannetons are indispensable tools for the bread baker and are sold at specialty kitchen and baking stores or online.

BAKER'S LAME

A baker's lame is a blade that is used to slice the surface of raw dough in order to control its expansion as it bakes. Use a baker's lame or a serrated knife to slice the surface of the Yeasted Loaf (page 71) and Baguettes (page 97).

THERMOMETERS

A probe thermometer is essential for monitoring the temperature of the flour as it is milled. It is also handy for monitoring a dough's temperature during the fermentation process to ensure it is within the suggested range. There are a number of recipes for which hitting a certain temperature range is essential, including the Sourdough Loaf, Sourdough Durum Loaf, Potato Rolls, and Whole Wheat Croissants. An oven thermometer is useful for calibrating home ovens (see page 115).

PASTA-MAKING TOOLS

The basic utensils for the pasta recipes are a rolling pin and a work surface. None of these recipes require special equipment, although if you wish to speed up the kneading process, you can do so by passing the dough through a pasta machine.

If you don't have a pasta wheel for cutting ravioli, use a cookie cutter or a sharp knife instead.

The doughs for Potato Gnocchi (page 150) and Passatelli (page 158) both call for a potato ricer.

A spray bottle or a brush is helpful for sealing ravioli and applying oil to some doughs.

AIRTIGHT CONTAINERS

Store wheat berries and milled flour in airtight containers to ensure maximum freshness.

INGREDIENTS

EGGS

Unless otherwise stated, my recipes call for large eggs. I recommend using farm-fresh organic eggs whenever possible. Some of the recipes list egg quantities in metric units. In cases where such precision isn't essential, the recipe simply lists the number of eggs. A whole large egg weighs approximately 60 grams; the yolk weighs about 20 grams and the white around 40 grams.

FILTERED WATER

Tap water can contain chlorine and/or fluoride and varies in mineral content and temperature. For the most consistent results, I always use filtered water.

OIL

Unless otherwise noted, always use extra-virgin olive oil. For greasing bowls and baking sheets, use this or any other neutral oil like grapeseed, canola, peanut, soybean, or corn.

SALT

Salt, which enhances flavor while taming fermentation, is an essential ingredient in doughs. Always use sea salt unless otherwise noted.

YEAST

Yeast is a single-cell fungus that can be culled from nature to make levain (page 90) or purchased in ready-to-use form. Fresh compact yeast and active dry yeast use the same fungus to ferment the dough. Fresh compact yeast, also known as cake yeast and fresh compressed yeast, has a small amount of water in it, so when you add it to the dough it blends easily. Active dry yeast, on the other hand, must be dissolved in water to be activated.

With all of this information, what you already have in your kitchen, and your curiosity and love for delicious food, you are ready to start your own Flour Lab!

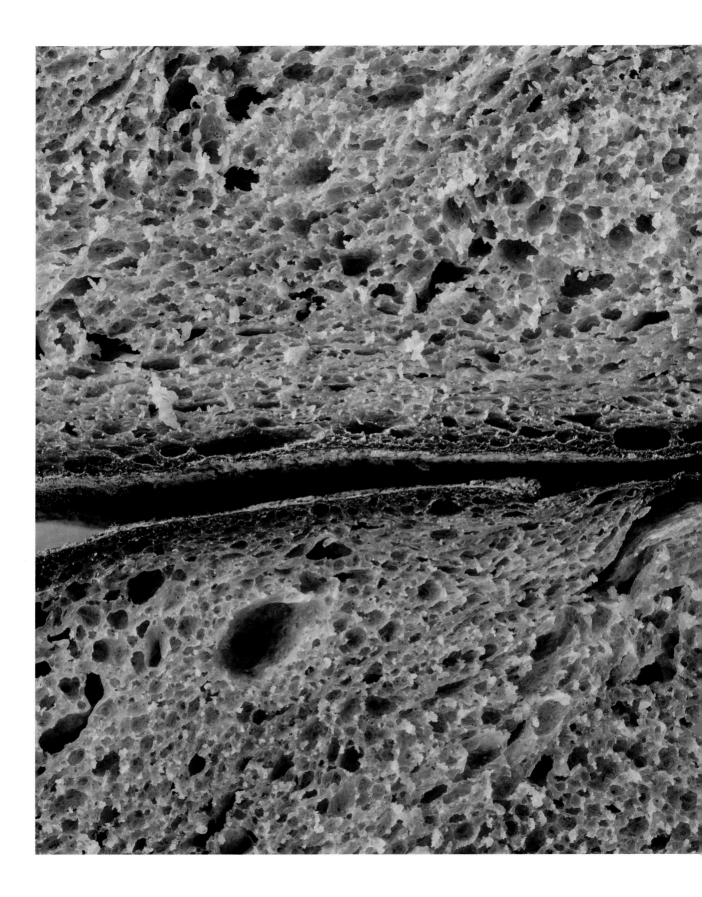

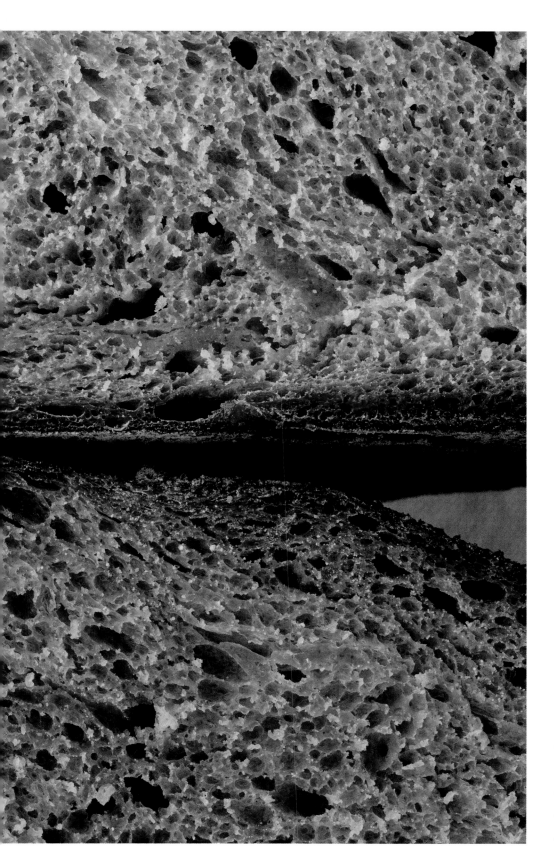

MAKING
BREAD

Bread is made from a few simple ingredients: flour, water, yeast, and salt. Anyone can make it and it's one of the oldest recipes on the planet. Perfecting bread, on the other hand, is a lifelong journey. Some days, I don't think about anything except bread and yet I never tire of the topic. The more time I spend milling flour, mixing and fermenting dough, and baking bread, the more I realize how much there still is to learn about this ancient food.

The way I see it, a chef who doesn't make bread is the dude at the gym who wails on his upper body but never does a leg day. Yet in my profession, baking and cooking are most often separated in the kitchen. I worked in food for more than ten years before ever baking a single loaf of bread. Since discovering the magic of it, I know all my cooking is better for it. Baking bread has given me the tools to understand how flour works to create structure and texture and how fermentation develops flavor, so when I run into challenges with laminated pastries or handmade pastas, I can refer to lessons learned in bread baking to make crucial improvements.

CHOOSING THE RIGHT GRAIN FOR THE JOB

When I first started baking bread, and well before I started milling, I was programmed to think that in order to make a viable product, the bread flour had to have 11.5% to 14% protein. While I was learning, I believed that number was fixed in stone and that protein was the deciding factor in choosing a flour. When baking bread, I would reach for a commercially milled "bread flour," which had the requisite protein content for making a consistent, if uninteresting, product.

A turning point came during a discussion with Jonathan Bethany-McDowell, then the resident baker at Washington State University's Bread Lab. By the way, go see him at his stellar bakery Seylou in Washington, DC. I asked him what he used for bread flour, and he replied, "There is no such thing as bread flour. There are flours that are better adapted to bread making than others. I can make bread with stuff that has 8% protein if it has high starch quality [see page 31], but I can't make bread with a durum that has 14% protein if the starch quality is weak." His ideas were something I had never considered. At this time, I was fixated on baking bread with a big, soft, open crumb—that is, inner structure—and judged my progress based on those characteristics. I then realized I had been limiting myself to what were just a small handful of bread's potential traits. I began playing around with new (to me) flours, and the resulting breads were incredibly flavorful. Pretty early into these experiments, I stopped thinking about crumb as the ultimate bread-baking benchmark. My Instagram "crumb porn" shots might have suffered, but I made up for it in the flavor of my breads and in an unquenchable enthusiasm for trying new grains.

Turning for a moment to the concept of protein: The percentage and quality of protein in a flour, as well as the quality of its starch, indicate the dough's potential to capture the carbon dioxide created during the fermentation process. Generally, a dough made with low-protein flour will have a more difficult time capturing CO_2 than a dough made with a high-protein flour. It follows that I can change a bread's characteristics based on the flour that I select. For example, if I want an airy structure and wide-open crumb, I would use a hard winter wheat like Kansas Turkey because its protein and starch quality (see page 42) are both high, so they can trap plenty of air. But Kansas Turkey is not known for great flavor, so if I want a tastier bread, I use a flavorful red winter wheat such as Red Fife or Warthog. Those have poorer protein and starch quality, resulting in a denser product with less trapped air. The resulting bread might not make my dream slice to eat slathered with butter—when I eat bread and butter I want something light so it doesn't fill me up at the dinner table—but a denser bread would be great for using as the vehicle for toppings like salted anchovies, which turn the bread from a snack into a dish.

MILLING FOR BREAD

When it comes to milling grain for bread, you have quite a few options for how coarse or fine you mill the grain. You can choose to work with flour ranging in fineness from powder to semolina. Some bakers don't like to bake with superfine flour, preferring coarser, more rustic Old World–style grinds. The appeal of coarser flour is twofold: European bread masters prefer a coarser grind, so people trained in that style choose it in order to pay homage to this ancient tradition; and coarser milling allows you to mill faster and cooler, preserving the nutrient integrity of the grain. "Modern" bakers, seeking to break with tradition, prefer to use superfine flour. If you choose to follow suit, you will need to adjust the amount of water in a recipe, as finer flour absorbs more water.

EXTRACTION

All the flour in this chapter is 100% inclusion (see page 30), so sifting is not necessary. The presence of all this bran in your flour will contribute to the flavor and nutrition of the bread.

MIXING AND KNEADING

Mixing is the step in which the bread's ingredients are initially combined; it precedes the fermentation process. When it comes to bread making, the mixing phase would perhaps be better named the "strengthening and incorporating through contact" phase. Okay, maybe that rebranding needs some work. But what I mean is, every time you touch the dough during the bread-making process, you are giving it strength. Mixing is just the first step in this process, encouraging the dough's structure to build gluten strands. That's why I start many of my breads with an autolyze (see page 31).

When mixing freshly milled flour with just water—or with water, salt, and yeast—by hand or by mixer I try to keep the time I spend mixing to a minimum. Oxidation is a major threat to flavor. As the mixture is exposed to oxygen, it begins to lose some of its flavor and nutrients. You can see evidence of oxidation in the color of the dough: the more you mix, the whiter it gets. Think of this as the exact opposite of an avocado, which browns as it is exposed to oxygen. To prevent oxidation in the fermentation phase, cover the dough with plastic wrap.

When the ingredients have been mixed, I build strength in the dough by stretching and pulling it. In colloquial terms, this might be called kneading, but don't think of this as the energetic two-hand kneading that is described in the pasta chapter. Rather, it is a series of pulling and stretching movements that helps the dough develop strength and helps build the gluten network.

FERMENTING

Fermentation, also known as "proofing," is the fundamental step that must occur for a dough to become bread and not simply pasta. During fermentation, yeast, in the form of either commercial yeast or levain, feeds on the flour's endosperm, leaving carbon dioxide and gluten strands in its wake. When a dough is made with freshly milled flour, the fermentation process is livelier because there are more nutrients in the flour and therefore more food and enzymes for the yeast to feed on. For this reason, you can ferment freshly milled flour doughs in the refrigerator instead of at a warm temperature. This cold fermentation produces greater flavor and lower acidity.

If you use commercial yeast, as opposed to levain, you have a greater range of grains to choose from. Commercial yeast is powerful and quickly gives strength to dough without your having to pay much attention. On the other hand, levain works more slowly and due to its acidity and length of fermentation, it "digests" the flour more as it ferments, increasing digestibility. This limits the types of flours that can be used because the flour must be able to tolerate longer fermentation but still retain properties that make for a good bake. While commercial yeast yields a more predictable, consistent product, levain offers the possibility of more flavor and complexity, both natural by-products of wild fermentation. Additionally, this kind of fermentation breaks down the wheat on a molecular level—predigestion if you will—into something that is more easily digested by the human gut. That's the beauty of wild yeast at work. With experience, you can harness the potential of levain and its wild yeasts to make unbelievably delicious and very digestible bread.

SHAPING

Shaping the dough, not to be confused with kneading, follows the fermentation process and offers a final opportunity to impart strength to a developing dough. The only dough that is not subjected to shaping is the Yeasted Ciabatta (page 77); we skip the shaping there in order to avoid disrupting that dough's delicate structure. If you knead or apply too much pressure to the deliberately overfermented ciabatta dough, it will collapse. For other bread doughs, you may notice that they are softer and more porridge-like than their conventional counterparts; this is because freshly milled flour holds more water. Some of the doughs are shaped on a watered surface rather than a floured one, which provides the benefit of not introducing unfermented flour into the dough. It's easier to work with very hydrated doughs on water but you do have to work more quickly to prevent the dough from becoming sticky.

BAKING

Bake times are longer for breads made with freshly milled flour because the loaves are denser, thanks to their greater concentration of nutrients, oils, and fibers. Additionally, the color of a dough made with freshly milled flour changes into vibrant and varied shades as it bakes, thanks again to the complexity of whole grains, which contain nutrients, oils, and fibers not present in commodity wheat. These components change color as they caramelize during baking.

AGING

Breads made with freshly milled flour benefit from aging, a process during which flavors not initially present are able to develop in the bread. The aromas of the fermented flour need time to permeate the loaf, so always let a loaf cool completely before slicing—and ideally wait until the next day to allow the aromas and flavors to mature. The bread interacts with its environment and changes as it oxidizes, much the way a bottle of wine does after it is opened to breathe. The flavors vary from bread to bread.

STORAGE

Moisture plays a role in keeping bread from becoming stale. Storing any kind of bread in a refrigerator will age the bread more rapidly than storing it on a counter, because refrigeration pulls moisture out of the bread more quickly. To keep bread fresh longer, store it in a brown paper bag or plastic wrap on your counter. Freezing is another great way to preserve bread. I wrap whole loaves in plastic wrap, freeze them, and defrost them at room temperature when I am ready to use them.

Home ovens reach 500°F to 550°F, and you can best harness this heat with a baking stone. A baking stone (see page 60) will give your bread a better crust, better volume, and incomparable lightness. For the best results, preheat the stone for at least 45 minutes before baking. The baking time depends upon your baking surface and will be shorter if you use a stone. Allow 10 to 15 minutes for the stone to return to the required temperature between bakes.

If you want to harness even more of your home oven's heat, preheat cast-iron pots and pans on the rack below the stone.

YEASTED LOAF

MAKES ONE 1,825-GRAM LOAF

Yeasted breads are made with commercially cultivated yeast—think of those packets of active dry yeast and cubes of fresh compact yeast that you buy at the supermarket. The yeast is created in a laboratory and consequently is easier and more reliable to work with than sourdough starter, also known as levain, which can be temperamental and requires careful attention to timing, dough temperatures, shaping, and numerous other variables. Too often, we are told that great artisanal bread *must* use a sourdough starter in order to be valid. That's simply not true. You can make a fabulously flavorful artisanal bread with commercial yeast and freshly milled flour, and this hard winter wheat Yeasted Loaf is proof. I like to use Red Fife flour for a lovely nutty flavor and wonderful aroma. Red Fife is a bit more difficult to work with than some other hard winter wheats because of its relatively low protein content, so if you're just getting started, use Kansas Turkey or Warthog instead. The dough cold-ferments overnight twice, so prepare the dough 2 days before you plan to bake the loaf.

800 grams water, warmed to 77°F

1,000 grams hard winter wheat flour (I like Red Fife)

25 grams sea salt

10 grams fresh compact yeast

Neutral oil (see page 62), for greasing

Rice Flour Mixture (page 74) or bench flour (see tip on page 138), for dusting

---

When mixing the flour and water, add the water to the bowl first to keep the flour from clumping and sticking to the bottom.

In the bowl of a stand mixer fitted with the dough hook, combine the water, flour, salt, and yeast. Mix on low speed until the flour is incorporated, about 1 minute. Cover the bowl with plastic wrap and set the dough aside to hydrate for 45 minutes. The dough's texture will change from rough to smooth as it rests.

Uncover the bowl and mix the dough on low speed for 4 minutes; then mix it on medium speed for 2 minutes. Transfer the dough to a medium oiled bowl, cover it with plastic wrap, and place it in the refrigerator to cold-ferment overnight.

With a bench scraper, loosen the dough from the sides of the bowl, then turn it out onto a work surface that you have brushed sparingly with water.

PRE-SHAPE THE DOUGH: See photographs on pages 83–85. With two wet hands slightly tilted downward, lift the dough from the middle and let it hang. The

dough will stretch as it hangs. Let the dough stretch down onto the work surface, then drop the middle part onto the resting hanging ends. Repeat the lifting, hanging, and dropping process once more.

Drag the dough across the surface toward you with both hands. Turn it 90 degrees and drag it again. Repeat the turning and dragging at least 4 and no more than 6 times, until you have a rough ball.

Set the dough aside, uncovered, for 1 hour to allow it to ferment at room temperature.

GIVE THE LOAF ITS FINAL SHAPE: See photographs on page 89. Sprinkle a light stripe of rice flour mixture or bench flour on your work surface. Dip the bottom of the dough into the flour, then transfer it to a clean surface. With floured fingertips, press into the surface of the dough, working vertically (down toward the work surface) from top to bottom, elongating the dough. Flip the bottom half of the dough

(recipe continues through page 75)

over the top half. Grab each side of the dough and stretch it gently to its limit; the dough will tell you how much it can stretch. Return it to the work surface. Fold one end to the center of the dough, then fold the other end over the folded dough. Working from the edge closest to you, roll the dough over itself. Drag the dough across the surface toward you with both hands to seal the seam. Transfer the dough, seam-side down, to a 2-kilogram banneton that you have dusted with rice flour mixture or bench flour.

Transfer the banneton, uncovered, to the refrigerator and let the dough ferment until it has increased in volume by 20%, about 24 hours.

TEST THE LOAF'S ACTIVITY: Gently press the loaf with one finger to see how it responds. If the indentation doesn't bounce back at all, it is ready to go in the oven. If the indentation bounces back just a little bit but you can still see it, it is ready to go in the oven. If the indentation bounces back quickly, your loaf has some strength left to give—proof it, uncovered, at room temperature for another 60 minutes.

Preheat the oven to 500°F and set a Dutch oven inside to preheat as well.

Place the preheated Dutch oven on a safe work surface (be sure to use oven mitts, as it will be very hot!), and carefully drop the dough into it. Score the surface with a baker's lame or a serrated knife to a depth of ⅛ inch. Cover the Dutch oven with a lid and return it to the oven.

After 10 minutes, remove the lid from the Dutch oven to release the steam. Reduce the temperature to 400°F and bake, uncovered, until the bread takes on a dark golden color, about 40 minutes more.

Remove the bread and allow it to cool completely on a wire rack before slicing it.

This bread will reach its height of fragrance after cooling down completely, or ideally the next day. Stored in a brown paper bag or wrapped in plastic wrap, it will stay fresh for up to 3 days on the counter; wrapped in plastic wrap, it will keep for up to 6 months in the freezer.

Bakers use rice flour or rice flour mixtures when dusting bannetons (baking baskets) because rice doesn't absorb water the same way flour does, allowing the dough to be removed from the banneton easily without sticking.

RICE FLOUR
MAKES 1 CUP

Use rice flour on your work surface for shaping loaves and for dusting a banneton for bread loaves or a *couche* for baguettes (see page 61).

175 grams (1 cup) rice (I like any cheap organic white rice)

Pass the rice through a burr mill, grinding it to the consistency of fine sand. The rice flour will keep in a sealed container at room temperature for up to 1 month.

RICE FLOUR MIXTURE
MAKES 2 CUPS

Use rice flour mixture to dust bannetons for proofing loaves.

1 recipe Rice Flour

65 grams (1 cup) bran

In a medium bowl, whisk together the rice flour and the bran. The mixture will keep in a sealed container at room temperature for up to 1 month.

YEASTED CIABATTA

MAKES FOUR 450-GRAM LOAVES

The first time I tried a ciabatta was at the fast-food restaurant Subway. To me, at the time, it was just bread, but when I went to Italy I learned it was so much more. The light and airy crumb sheathed in a super-thin crust suddenly seemed like an unadorned pizza gone a bit crazy. The holes were big and open and numerous. It might seem that I was late to the ciabatta party, but if you think about it, ciabatta was late to the bread party. It was just invented in the twentieth century to be a quick and simple sandwich bread. Unlike historic breads, which can have tremendous flavor, even a great ciabatta can be fairly bland since it's basically a vehicle for fillings.

The way I came to this recipe was unexpected. I wasn't aiming for a ciabatta at all. During the 2016 Snowpocalypse, the second biggest blizzard in New York City's history, I couldn't get to the Bread Lab for days. The dough for our Yeasted Loaf was trapped in the walk-in refrigerator, fermenting, for a week. When we finally got in, the dough was so wet and sticky that we couldn't even shape it; so we took a chance, sliced it up, and baked it off. What was the worst that could happen? What did happen was delicious; when we baked it, it turned into a really tasty, supremely light ciabatta.

Due to the high hydration (90%), this dough can be challenging for beginners. But a ciabatta doesn't have to be perfectly shaped, so don't worry if it looks like a wonky mess. I make ciabatta with hard winter wheat and typically reach for Magog, a grain that isn't naturally strong but builds strength through a long fermentation to earn a nice open crumb. The dough ferments for 72 hours, so plan ahead if you don't think a blizzard is on the way.

900 grams water, warmed to 77°F

1,000 grams hard winter wheat flour (I like Magog)

25 grams sea salt

10 grams fresh compact yeast

Neutral oil (see page 62), for greasing

Bench flour (see tip on page 138), for dusting

Ciabatta dough is very similar to that of the Yeasted Loaf (page 71) but has greater hydration. Comparing the two doughs is a good exercise in seeing how hydration affects dough development and how one bread can become another by making slight adjustments to the ingredient proportions, even when all the ingredients themselves are the same.

In the bowl of a stand mixer fitted with the dough hook, combine the water, flour, salt, and yeast. Mix on low speed until the flour is incorporated, about 1 minute. Cover the bowl with plastic wrap and set the dough aside to hydrate for 45 minutes. The dough's texture will change from rough to smooth as it rests.

Uncover the bowl and mix on low speed for 4 minutes; then mix on medium speed for 2 minutes. Transfer the dough to a medium oiled bowl, cover it with plastic wrap, and place the dough in the refrigerator to cold-ferment for about 72 hours.

(recipe continues through page 79)

Preheat the oven to 500°F and set a baking stone or inverted baking sheet in the oven to preheat as well.

With a bench scraper, loosen the dough from the sides of the bowl and turn it out onto a liberally floured work surface, trying to maintain the shape of the bowl. Generously dust the surface of the dough and your bench scraper with more bench flour. Cut the dough into 4 equal pieces, slicing decisively to decrease the risk of collapse (1, 2). Coax each piece into a rectangle by gently pushing the dough into the desired shape.

Transfer one piece of the dough to a pizza peel that has been dusted with bench flour or a parchment-lined inverted baking sheet that has been dusted with bench flour. Give it a gentle push with your fingertips, working vertically from one edge of the dough to the other (3, 4), and set it aside at room temperature to proof for 15 minutes.

Transfer the piece of dough to the preheated baking stone or inverted baking sheet. If using a parchment-lined baking sheet as a peel, slide the dough and parchment together onto the preheated surface. Bake until the ciabatta is a light golden color, about 17 minutes.

Allow the ciabatta to cool completely on a wire rack before slicing. Repeat with the remaining dough.

The bread will reach its height of fragrance after cooling down completely, or ideally the next day. Stored in a brown paper bag or wrapped in plastic wrap, it keeps well for up to 3 days on the counter; or wrapped in plastic wrap, it will keep for up to 6 months in the freezer.

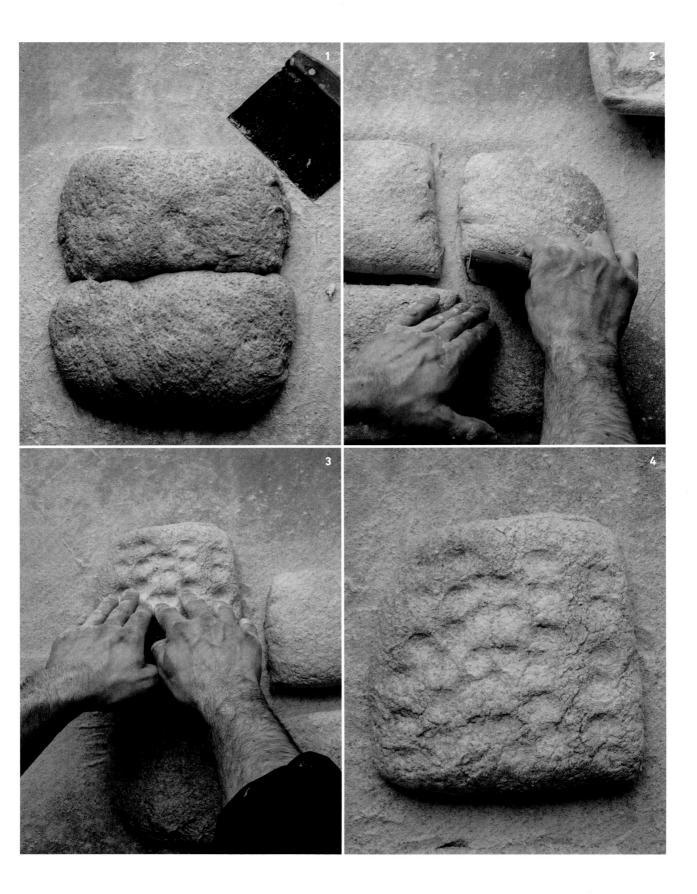

SOURDOUGH LOAF

MAKES TWO 1-KILOGRAM LOAVES

When I was running the Brooklyn Bread Lab, this was the dough that I would teach to students who came to Bushwick to learn bread making. I have a few sourdough loaves in my arsenal, but what's special about this one is how the larger than normal amount of levain (compared with a classic sourdough recipe), coupled with a long cold fermentation, tames the dough's acidity and teases out great flavors from the grain. When it comes to shaping, I prefer minimum contact with this dough, allowing it to build strength through slowly fermenting, which gives the bread a soft crumb. You can use any hard red winter wheat you like, but I prefer Warthog for this loaf because it is inexpensive, full of flavor, and easy to find at farmers' markets on the East Coast, where I was doing the majority of my baking. Specialty shops and the internet can help you track it down elsewhere. The dough ferments for 4 to 6 hours at room temperature, then in the refrigerator overnight.

800 grams water, warmed to 77°F

1,000 grams hard red winter wheat flour (I like Warthog)

200 grams Levain (page 90)

25 grams sea salt

Rice Flour Mixture (page 74), for dusting

FERMENTATION

Higher temperatures cause bread to ferment faster at the cost of flavor, while lower temperatures contribute to a slower rise and more complex flavors—that's why I subject so many of my doughs to a cold ferment in the refrigerator before baking. When I say "room temperature," I always mean 71°F to 77°F. With a bit of tweaking to adapt to your environment, you should be able to reproduce any of my doughs just about anywhere.

In a large bowl, mix the water and flour together with a wooden spoon just until incorporated. Cover the bowl with plastic wrap and set the dough aside to hydrate for 45 minutes.

Uncover the bowl, add the levain and the salt, and mix. With one wet hand, lightly grasp one edge of the dough. Pull this flap upward and outward, then attach it to the top of the dough. Give the bowl a one-eighth turn and repeat the pulling and attaching. Continue with one-eighth turns until all of the salt has been incorporated, 3 to 4 minutes. If the salt has not dissolved after this time, add 50 to 100 grams of water to help the salt dissolve, and then continue with one-eighth turns until all of the salt has been incorporated.

Use a thermometer to test the dough; it should be 75°F to 77°F, slightly cooler than your hands. If it is not, move the dough to a warmer part of your kitchen and let it sit there until it reaches the desired temperature range and becomes smooth.

When the dough is smooth, cover the bowl with plastic wrap and allow the dough to ferment at room temperature until you see a tiny bit of bubbling on its surface and the dough starts to relax, about 1 hour.

Uncover the bowl, and with two wet hands slightly tilted downward, lift the dough from the middle (1, 2) and let it hang (3). The dough will stretch as it hangs. Let the dough stretch, then drop the middle part onto the resting hanging ends (4). This step builds strength in the dough. Cover the bowl again with plastic wrap and set it aside to let the dough ferment for 1 hour. Then repeat the lifting, hanging, and dropping process 2 more times, allowing 1 hour of fermenting after each session, including the final one.

After the dough has fermented for that final hour, fill a deep container with water. Moisten your hands and a plastic bench scraper. With the scraper, loosen the dough from the sides of the bowl, then turn it out onto a surface sparingly brushed with water.

(recipe continues through page 93)

Cut the dough in half with the bench scraper or a sharp knife.

PRE-SHAPE THE DOUGH: With two wet hands slightly tilted downward, lift one of the dough pieces from the middle (1, 2) and let it hang. The dough will stretch as it hangs (3). Let the dough stretch onto the work surface, then drop the middle part onto the resting hanging ends (4, 5). Repeat the lifting, hanging, and dropping process once more.

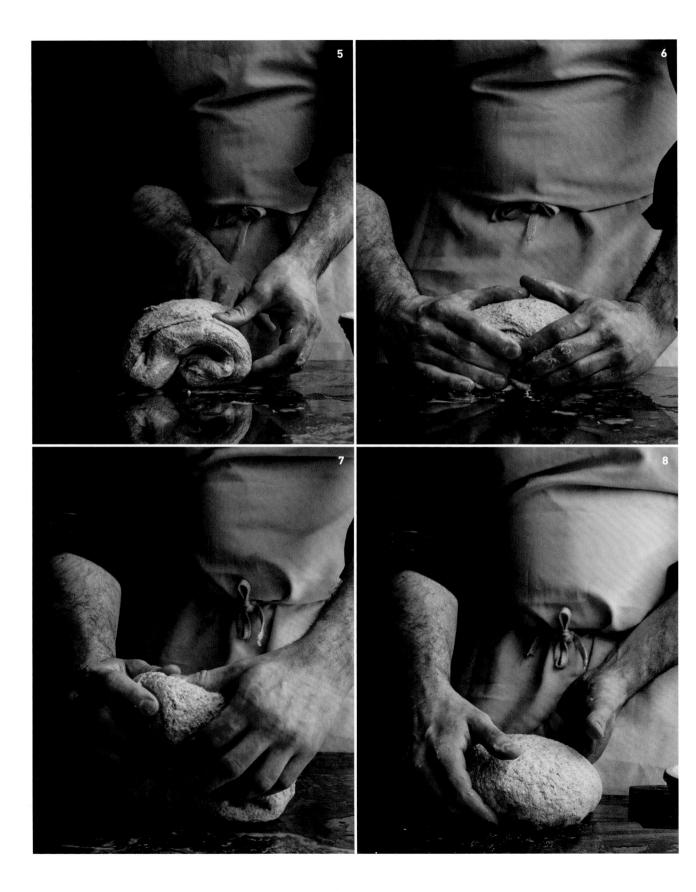

Drag the dough across the surface toward you with both hands (6). Turn it 90 degrees (7) and drag it again. Repeat the turning and dragging at least 4 and no more than 6 times, until you have a rough ball (8). Repeat with the second piece of dough. Set both aside to ferment at room temperature, uncovered, for 1 hour.

GIVE THE LOAVES THEIR FINAL
SHAPE: Sprinkle a light stripe of
rice flour mixture on your work
surface. Dip the bottom of each
piece of dough into the flour, and
transfer them to a clean surface.
With floured fingertips, press into
the surface of one piece of dough,
working vertically (down toward
the work surface) from top to
bottom, elongating the dough.

Flip the bottom half of the dough over the top half (9). Grab each side of the dough and stretch it gently to its limit (10); the dough will tell you how much it can stretch. Return it to the work surface. Fold one end to the center of the dough, then fold the other end over the folded dough (11). Working from the edge closest to you, roll the dough over itself (12). Drag the dough across the surface toward you (13) with both hands to seal the seam (14). Transfer the dough, seam-side down, to a 1-kilogram banneton dusted with rice flour mixture. Repeat with the second piece of dough.

If the dough is very active and bubbly, immediately place the uncovered shaped loaves in the refrigerator and let them proof overnight. If the dough isn't very bubbly and doesn't feel active, allow it to sit at room temperature, uncovered, for 1 hour, and then place the loaves in the refrigerator to ferment overnight.

TEST THE LOAVES' ACTIVITY: Gently press the loaves with one finger to see how they respond. If the indentation doesn't bounce back at all, they are ready to go in the oven. If the indentation bounces back just a little bit but you can still see it, they are ready to go in the oven. If the indentation bounces back quickly, your loaves have some strength left to give—proof them, uncovered, at room temperature for another 60 minutes.

Preheat the oven to 500°F and set a Dutch oven inside to preheat as well.

Place the preheated Dutch oven on a safe work surface (be sure to use oven mitts, as it will be very hot!), and carefully drop one piece of the dough into it. Score the surface with a baker's lame or serrated knife to a depth of ⅛ inch. Cover the Dutch oven with a lid and return it to the oven.

After 10 minutes, remove the lid from the Dutch oven to release the steam. Reduce the temperature to 400°F and bake, uncovered, until the bread takes on a dark golden color, about 40 minutes more. (Begin checking for doneness at the 30-minute mark.)

Unmold the bread, and allow it to cool completely on a wire rack before slicing it. Bake the second piece of dough, allowing the oven and the Dutch oven to return to 500°F before baking.

This bread will reach its height of fragrance after cooling down completely, or ideally the next day. Stored in a brown paper bag or wrapped in plastic wrap, it will stay fresh for 3 days at room temperature; wrapped in plastic wrap, it will keep for up to 6 months in the freezer.

LEVAIN

MAKES 125 GRAMS LEVAIN

Levain, also known as sourdough starter, is a flour and water mixture that has been left out in the open to ferment naturally. The yeasts and bacteria that live in the air land in the mixture and begin to reproduce there along with the yeast and bacteria naturally present in the flour. Levain is used in bread making to ferment dough.

People care deeply about their levain. Romance and nostalgia are often caught up in stories of where it came from and who developed it. I recall an Italian *pizzaiolo* telling me his levain (he called it *lievito madre*, "mother yeast") was from a bakery in Puglia and dated back to the 1930s. He was head over heels. I feel a little differently about ancient levain. I don't want to fall in love with a fungus-infected flour mixture, which is essentially what it is. I want to use it as a tool to make a delicious bread. The reality is, levain is made up of the ambient yeast from its surroundings and it is completely susceptible to the nature of its environment. So as fun as it is to brag about having a nearly-100-year-old levain from Italy, the moment you move a levain to a new environment, it starts to be populated by local yeasts, and they conquer and replace the old ones—nothing romantic about it! So if your levain has spent even a few days in NYC, it has become a full-blown New Yorker.

So the key to a stellar levain isn't getting it from a historical source or a favorite place, but rather letting it develop in your home or restaurant or bakery kitchen and allowing it to reflect the location's terroir. Terroir comes into play with the amount of levain, too: If I'm in a tropical climate, I would use a lot less than specified in a recipe because of the warm and humid conditions, an environment in which yeast naturally thrives. On the other hand, if I am in my home state of Maine, I may add more than is recommended due to the cooler, drier climate, which slows the yeast down. *That's* what is thrilling and romantic to me about levain: the way it reacts to its environment in a tangible way.

When starting a new levain, I always begin with rye flour because rye berries are naturally rich in yeast, and therefore a starter made with rye flour will be more active than one made with another grain. Once the starter gets going, I can swap out the rye flour for just about any flour but durum. About 3 days before I plan to use a levain, I substitute for the rye flour the flour I intend to make the recipe with, using the same amount of flour as the rye.

Be sure to begin your levain at least 4 days before using it in a recipe. As long as the levain has been properly fed and is active, it can be used forever.

500 grams soft or hard wheat flour

500 grams rye flour

In a large resealable container, combine the flours.

In a small glass bowl, combine 100 grams of room-temperature water and 100 grams of the flour mixture, and stir until smooth. (Place the remaining flour mixture in the refrigerator.) Cover the bowl with a clean kitchen towel and allow the mixture to sit at warm room temperature (72°F to 75°F) to ferment for 48 hours.

Check the mixture for signs of fermentation, such as bubbles on the surface and around the edges of the bowl. Cover it again with a clean kitchen towel and allow it to sit for another 24 hours.

Check that the bubbling has intensified. You will be able to smell the wonderfully musty and acidic aromas of fermentation. If you cannot, discard the mixture and begin again.

Place 25 grams of the fermented starter in a small bowl, discarding the remainder. Add 50 grams of room-temperature water and 50 grams of the reserved flour mixture, and mix well. Cover the bowl with a clean kitchen towel and allow it to sit at warm room temperature for 24 hours. Repeat the process, using 25 grams of the starter mixture, adding 50 grams each of the water and flour mixture, and allowing it to ferment for 24 hours.

When the levain is active, begin repeating the feeding cycle every 12 hours, always combining 25 grams of the starter mixture with 50 grams each of the water and flour mixture. You will observe the rise-and-fall cycle: the volume will increase after feeding, then decrease. The aromas will change as well: at first funky and acidic, followed by pleasantly sour, reminiscent of yogurt. On the day before you plan to use the levain, feed it twice, 12 hours apart, on a schedule that puts the starter in its most active phase at the time you plan to use it.

To make any of the breads in this chapter, make the last two feedings before baking with whatever flour is called for in the recipe. If the recipe calls for two types of flour, use both in the same proportions in which they appear in the recipe.

CHANGING THE HYDRATION
You can change the hydration of levain, which comes in handy for breads made with durum or other flours that break down in the presence of excess water. To make a 90% levain for the Sourdough Durum Loaf (page 94), place 50 grams of the slurry-textured starter in a small bowl and add 50 grams of room-temperature water and 110 grams of the flour mixture. Knead it into a smooth dough. Cover the bowl with plastic wrap and allow the dough to ferment at room temperature for 12 hours. The signs of activity are identical for this 90% hydration levain and a 100% one.

Place 50 grams of the fermented starter in a small bowl, discarding the remainder. Add 50 grams of room-temperature water and 110 grams of the flour mixture.

Repeat the feeding and discarding process every 12 hours for about 1 week. You will observe the rise-and-fall cycle.

SCALING UP THE RECIPE
If you have a small amount of levain, you can make more by scaling up the recipe, adjusting the discarding and feeding amounts proportionally. For example, to make 200 grams of levain for the Sourdough Loaf (page 81), combine 100 grams of levain with 100 grams of water and 100 grams of flour in a large glass jar and stir until incorporated. Set it aside at warm room temperature to mature for 4 hours, or until doubled in size, before using. This will give you a total of 300 grams of active levain: 200 for the Sourdough Loaf and 100 to continue feeding for other recipes.

MAINTAINING YOUR LEVAIN
Continue the feeding and discarding process every 12 hours. If you're not using it for a few days or can't feed your levain on the suggested schedule, you can slow down the fermentation through refrigeration. First, feed the levain normally, leave it for 2 hours at room temperature, then transfer it, covered, to the refrigerator. You can feed the levain this way every 48 hours. Just be sure to complete at least two 12-hour room-temperature feeding cycles prior to using the levain.

SOURDOUGH DURUM LOAF

MAKES TWO 1,100-GRAM LOAVES

This sourdough bread uses a mixture of durum wheat and Warthog flours with a 90% hydration levain. The hydration of normal levain is a full 100%, so this one is drier than average. Drier levain ferments more slowly and is more stable temperature-wise. I use a reduced-hydration levain because durum breaks down with water, so using less water overall in the recipe helps the durum maintain its integrity. The dough ferments for 4 to 6 hours at room temperature, then in the refrigerator overnight.

830 grams water, warmed to 77°F

800 grams durum wheat flour

200 grams hard red winter wheat flour (I like Warthog)

510 grams 90% hydration Warthog levain (see page 91)

27 grams sea salt

Rice Flour (page 74), for dusting

Rice Flour Mixture (page 74) or bench flour (see tip on page 138), for dusting

---

When there are two or more loaves or pizzas in a recipe, I suggest baking one at a time (unless otherwise stated), which is best for home ovens. If you have a professional oven, you can get away with baking off a lot of items at once.

In the bowl of a stand mixer fitted with the dough hook, combine the water, the durum flour, Warthog flour, levain, and salt. Mix on low speed until the flour is incorporated, about 1 minute. Cover the bowl with plastic wrap and set the dough aside to hydrate for 45 minutes. The dough's texture will change from rough to smooth as it rests.

Uncover the bowl and mix the dough on low speed for 4 minutes; then mix it on medium speed for 2 minutes. Cover the bowl with plastic wrap and set it aside to let the dough ferment at room temperature for 1 hour.

Use a thermometer to test the dough; it should be 75°F to 77°F, slightly cooler than your hands. If it is not, move the dough to a warmer part of your kitchen and leave it there until it reaches the desired temperature range.

When the dough is smooth, cover the bowl with plastic wrap and allow the dough to ferment at room temperature until you see a tiny bit of bubbling on its surface and the dough starts to relax, about 1 hour.

Uncover the bowl, and with two wet hands slightly tilted downward, lift the dough from the middle and let it hang. The dough will stretch down as it hangs. Let the dough stretch,

then drop the middle part onto the resting hanging ends. Cover the bowl again with plastic wrap, and set it aside at room temperature to ferment for 1 hour. Repeat the lifting, hanging, and dropping process 2 more times, allowing 1 hour of fermenting after each session, including the final one.

Cut the dough in half with a bench scraper or a sharp knife.

PRE-SHAPE THE DOUGH: With two wet hands, take one dough piece and repeat the lifting, hanging, and dropping process twice. Drag the dough across the surface toward you with both hands. Turn it 90 degrees and drag it again. Repeat the turning and dragging at least 4 and no more than 6 times, until you have a rough ball. Repeat with the second piece of dough. Set both aside to allow them to ferment at room temperature, uncovered, for 1 hour.

GIVE THE LOAVES THEIR FINAL SHAPE: Sprinkle a light stripe of rice flour on your work surface. Dip the bottom of each piece of dough into the flour, then transfer them to a clean surface. With floured fingertips, press into the surface of one piece of dough, working vertically (down toward the work surface) from top to bottom, elongating the dough. Flip the bottom half of the dough over the top half. Grab each side of the dough and stretch it gently to its limit; the dough will tell you how much it can stretch. Return it to the work surface. Fold one end to the center of the dough, then fold the other end over the folded dough. Working from the edge closest to you, roll the dough over itself. Drag the dough across the surface toward you with both hands to seal the seam. Transfer the dough, seam-side down, to a 1-kilogram banneton dusted with rice flour mixture or bench flour. Repeat with the second piece of dough.

Transfer the loaves to the refrigerator and allow them to proof, uncovered, at 41°F for 24 hours.

TEST THE LOAVES' ACTIVITY: Gently press the loaves with one finger to see how they respond. If the indentation doesn't bounce back at all, they are ready to go in the oven. If the indentation bounces back just a little bit but you can still see it, they are ready to go in the oven. If the indentation bounces back quickly, your loaves have some strength left to give—proof them, uncovered, at room temperature for another 60 minutes.

Preheat the oven to 500°F and set a Dutch oven inside to preheat as well.

Place the preheated Dutch oven on a safe work surface (be sure to use oven mitts, as it will be very hot!), and carefully drop one piece of the dough into it, seam-side down. Score the surface with a baker's lame or serrated knife to a depth of ⅛ inch. Cover the Dutch oven with a lid and return it to the oven.

After 10 minutes, remove the lid from the Dutch oven to release the steam. Reduce the temperature to 400°F and bake, uncovered, until the bread takes on a dark golden color, about 40 minutes more.

Unmold the bread, and allow it to cool completely on a wire rack before slicing it. Bake the second piece of dough, allowing the oven and Dutch oven to return to 500°F before baking.

This bread will reach its height of fragrance after cooling down completely, or ideally the next day. Stored in a brown paper bag or wrapped in plastic wrap, it will stay fresh for 3 days at room temperature; wrapped in plastic wrap, it will keep for up to 6 months in the freezer.

BAGUETTES

MAKES TWO 18-INCH BAGUETTES

When Melissa Rodriguez was promoted to executive chef at Del Posto, the critically acclaimed Italian fine-dining restaurant in Manhattan's Meatpacking District, one of the first things she sought to update was the restaurant's bread service. She tapped me to create a mini-baguette that would be adorned with a schmear of fresh cheese. Melissa wanted a mellow-tasting flour for the bread, so we settled on Redeemer wheat from Small Valley Milling in Pennsylvania. With high protein and medium flavor, this all-around performer makes a strong bread; mixing it with Sonora soft wheat lends softness. A small amount of levain, a small amount of *biga*, and a small amount of cake yeast give a pleasant balance of sourness, interior crumb, volume, and good shelf life. The malt syrup promotes fermentation activity by adding simple sugar to the dough for the yeast to eat. It also gives color to the bread. This recipe makes two full-size loaves, but feel free to play around with smaller shapes, Del Posto–style.

156 grams water, warmed to 77°F

97 grams hard red winter wheat flour (I like Redeemer)

156 grams soft wheat flour (I like Sonora)

6 grams bran

4 grams malt syrup

104 grams Levain (page 90)

104 grams cold *Biga* (page 102)

2 grams cake yeast

8 grams sea salt

Bench flour (see tip on page 138), for dusting

Durum semolina, for dusting

———————————

If you have a professional refrigerator and can adjust its temperature, ferment the dough at 46°F for 18 hours instead of 24 hours at 41°F. It will take only 1 hour for the temperature of the dough to come to room temperature if it is fermented at 46°F.

In the bowl of a stand mixer fitted with the dough hook, combine the water, hard red wheat flour, soft wheat flour, bran, and malt. Mix on low speed until the flour is incorporated, about 1 minute. Cover the bowl with plastic wrap and set it aside to let the dough hydrate for 45 minutes.

Uncover the bowl and add the levain, *biga*, yeast, and salt. Mix the dough for 4 minutes on low speed; then mix it on medium speed for 2 minutes. Use a thermometer to test the dough; it should be 75°F to 77°F, slightly cooler than your hands. If it is not, move the dough to a warmer part of your kitchen and let it sit there until it reaches the desired temperature range.

Cover the bowl with plastic wrap and set it aside to let the dough ferment at room temperature for 2 hours.

Uncover the bowl. With a bench scraper, loosen the dough from the sides of the bowl; then turn it out onto a lightly floured surface. Halve the dough with the bench scraper (1) or a sharp knife and gently coax each piece into a wide rectangle.

PRE-SHAPE THE DOUGH: Working with one piece of dough, fold the end farthest from you a third of the way down its length (2). Then fold the folded part over the open part (3). Repeat with the second piece of dough. Set them aside, uncovered, to rest for 20 minutes (4).

(recipe continues through page 103)

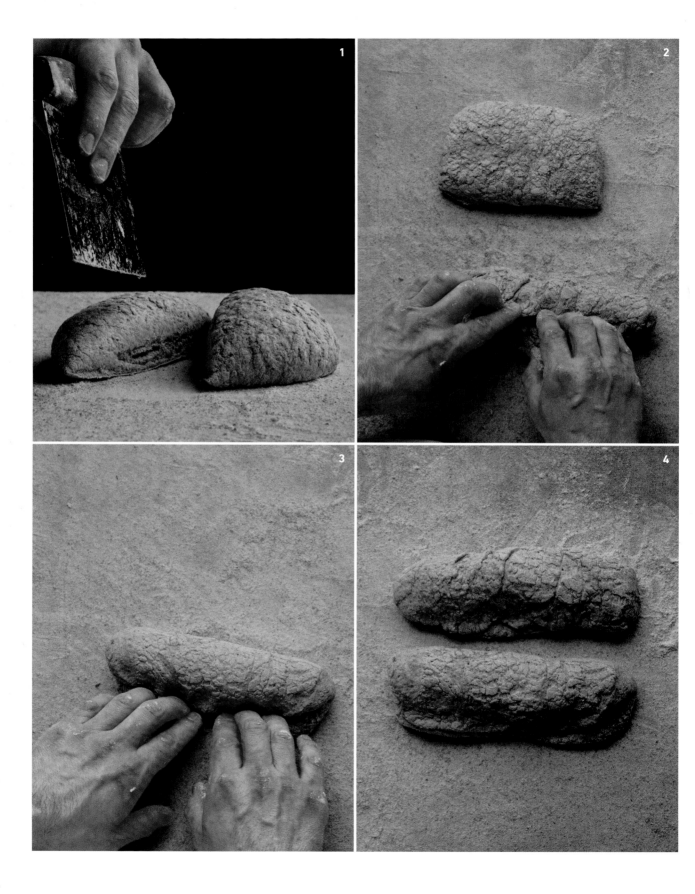

ROLL OUT THE DOUGH: Starting at one end of one piece of dough, fold a diagonal part over the dough and pinch and roll. Roll the dough tightly toward you, forcing the seam-side down. With your hands and palms, roll the dough out to 18 inches in length, keeping the seam down and pressing softly as you roll (5). With the heel of your palm, press with a bit more pressure to make a tapered end (6, 7). Repeat with the second piece of dough.

Prepare two 18 × 24-inch *couches* (see page 61). Lift a piece of dough, gripping it gently with two fingers, about 2 inches from each end and place it, seam-side up, in one of the *couche* valleys. Press the *couche* against the dough. Repeat with the

second piece of dough. Transfer the *couches* to the refrigerator, uncovered, and allow the dough to cold-ferment for at least 12 and up to 24 hours. The dough will become airy as it ferments.

Preheat the oven to 475°F and set a baking stone or inverted baking sheet in the oven to preheat as well.

Using the *couche* as a handle, transfer one piece of the dough, seam-side down, to a peel dusted with semolina. With a baker's lame or a serrated knife, and following the angle of the tapered end, make a diagonal incision 3 inches long and ⅛ inch deep, beginning at the height of its full thickness. Repeat 4 more times, beginning 1 inch from

the beginning of the first taper (2 inches in from the end of the incision). Repeat with the second piece of dough. Transfer both to the preheated baking stone and bake until the loaves take on a dark golden color, about 22 minutes.

Allow the baguettes to cool completely on a wire rack before slicing.

The baguettes will reach their height of fragrance and flavor after 24 hours. Stored in a brown paper bag or wrapped in plastic wrap, they will stay fresh for 3 days at room temperature; wrapped in plastic wrap, they will keep for up to 6 months in the freezer.

BIGA

MAKES 470 GRAMS BIGA

Biga, which functions as active yeast, must be made before you plan to use it. *Biga* is a type of "pre-ferment" in baking terms. Think of it as the cousin of levain, a sourdough starter made from flour, water, and the yeast naturally occurring in the environment. Like levain (see page 90), *biga* gives dough a more complex flavor and greater strength. But unlike sourdough starter, *biga* uses a bit of active dry yeast to help the fermentation get going.

192 grams water, warmed to 77°F

275 grams hard winter wheat flour (I like Redeemer)

3 grams active dry yeast

Neutral oil (see page 62), for greasing

Pour the water into the bowl of a stand mixer fitted with the dough hook. Add the flour, then the yeast. Mix on medium speed for 5 minutes. The dough should be fairly dry.

Transfer the *biga* to a lightly oiled medium bowl, cover it with plastic wrap, and allow the dough to ferment at room temperature overnight.

Check for signs of fermentation, such as bubbles on the surface and around the edges of the mixture. It is ready to be used immediately or can be stored in a sealed container in the refrigerator for up to 2 days.

POTATO ROLLS
MAKES ABOUT 40 POTATO ROLLS

Potato rolls, also known as "house rolls" in the Northeast, are a series of attached rolls that rise together and are baked together—think of a classic burger bun. This recipe is based on one from photographer and friend Caitlin Ochs's grandmother. I adapted her German potato roll recipe to accommodate freshly milled flour and the results were incredible (*danke, Grossmutter!*). The Sonora guarantees a delicate structure, while the rye gives great flavor. I like to serve these rolls as dessert, glazing them in honey and butter, with fresh fruit alongside, but they are also great as sandwich bread for pulled pork, brisket, or burgers.

187 grams water, warmed to 77°F

112 grams full-fat sour cream

90 grams egg yolks (about 10 yolks)

127 grams unsalted butter, softened

75 grams sugar

26 grams sea salt

675 grams soft spring wheat flour (I like Sonora), plus more for dusting

75 grams rye flour

210 grams 80% hydration levain (see page 91)

4 grams fresh compact yeast

25 grams honey (I like chestnut honey)

11 grams malt

412 grams potatoes, boiled, cooled, peeled, and cut into 1-inch cubes (I like Yukon Gold)

Neutral oil (see page 62), for greasing and brushing

3 whole eggs, beaten

Honey Butter (optional; recipe follows)

In the bowl of a stand mixer fitted with the dough hook, combine the water, sour cream, egg yolks, butter, sugar, salt, soft spring wheat flour, rye flour, levain, yeast, honey, and malt. Mix on low speed for 4 minutes and then on medium speed for 2 minutes.

Add the potatoes and mix on low speed until smooth, about 1 minute. Use a thermometer to test the dough; it should be 75°F to 77°F, slightly cooler than your hands. If it is not, move the dough to a warmer part of your kitchen and let it sit there until it reaches the desired temperature range.

Cover the bowl with plastic wrap and place it in the refrigerator to cold-ferment the dough.

Uncover the bowl. With a bench scraper, loosen the dough from the sides of the bowl; then turn it out onto a lightly floured surface. With the bench scraper or a sharp knife, cut the dough into 40 approximately 50-gram pieces (1).

Place the palm of your hand on top of one piece of dough, resting your thumb and pinkie against the sides and your other fingertips on the counter (2). Gently move the ball in circles, taking care to prevent any tears, to form a sphere. Repeat this process with the remaining dough.

Brush a baking sheet with neutral oil (3). Place the shaped dough balls on the sheet so that they are touching. Brush lightly with neutral oil and cover the whole baking sheet with plastic wrap. Set it aside for the rolls to ferment at room temperature until they have doubled in size, about 90 minutes.

Preheat the oven to 325°F.

TEST THE ROLLS' ACTIVITY: Gently press one of the rolls with one finger to see how it responds. If the indentation doesn't bounce back at all, the rolls are ready to go in the oven. If the indentation bounces back just a little bit but you can still see it, they are ready to go in the oven. If the indentation bounces back quickly, your rolls have some strength left to give—proof them, covered, at room temperature for another 30 to 60 minutes.

Brush the rolls with the beaten eggs (4) and bake until dark golden brown, about 45 minutes.

Use the rolls for sandwiches, or brush them all over with honey butter to serve them as dessert. Serve warm.

(recipe continues through page 107)

HONEY BUTTER

MAKES 1 ⅓ CUPS

65 grams (⅓ cup) unsalted butter

340 grams (1 cup) honey (I like chestnut honey)

Melt the butter in a small saucepan over low heat. Transfer it to a medium bowl and add the honey. Mix well.

BAGELS

MAKES 18 BAGELS

I had never made a bagel before I worked at the Brooklyn Bread Lab. Fortunately, I had bagel-loving baker Josh Pickins on my team and they are one of his favorite things to make. We wanted to create a bagel for hotel guests who were coming to Williamsburg for a classic Brooklyn experience, so we really had to nail it. We experimented with lard, duck fat, and chicken fat doughs. We tried vegetarian and vegan options. After some very intense deliberation and a not insignificant amount of bagel-fueled weight gain, we settled on a duck fat dough that has the chewiness of a New York bagel with the bready texture and soft open crumb of a Montreal-style bagel. The dough ferments in the refrigerator overnight, so prepare it the day before you plan to bake the bagels.

740 grams water, warmed to 77°F

1,000 grams hard red winter wheat flour (I like Redeemer)

250 grams Levain (page 90)

75 grams duck fat

1,050 grams malt syrup: 30 grams for the dough, 1,020 grams (3 cups) for the malt water

25 grams sea salt

2 grams fresh compact yeast

Rice flour (see page 74), for dusting

Neutral oil (see page 62), for greasing and brushing

The pH of sourdough products is low, or acidic. Acid is a natural preservative and consequently the acidity of sourdough products keeps them fresh.

In the bowl of a stand mixer fitted with the dough hook, combine the water, flour, levain, duck fat, and the 30 grams malt syrup. Mix on low speed until the flour is incorporated, about 1 minute. Cover the bowl with plastic wrap and set it aside to let the dough hydrate for 45 minutes.

Uncover the bowl and add the salt and yeast. Mix the dough on low speed for 4 minutes; then mix on medium speed for 2 minutes. Cover the bowl with plastic wrap and set it aside to let the dough ferment at room temperature for 3 hours. The dough will increase in volume by about 30%.

Uncover the bowl. With a bench scraper, loosen the dough from the sides of the bowl and turn it out onto a surface lightly dusted with rice flour. With the bench scraper or a sharp knife, divide the dough into 18 approximately 115-gram (4-ounce) pieces.

Place the palm of your hand on top of one piece of dough, resting your thumb and pinkie against the sides and your other fingertips on the counter (1). Gently move the ball in circles, taking care to prevent any tears, to form a sphere. Repeat this process with the remaining dough.

Place the shaped dough balls on greased baking sheets, spacing them about 4 inches apart. Brush them lightly with neutral oil and cover the baking sheets with plastic wrap. Place them in the refrigerator to cold-ferment until the dough is soft and airy, 12 hours or overnight.

Preheat the oven to 500°F and set a baking stone or inverted baking sheet in the oven to preheat as well.

While the oven is heating, set the baking sheets from the refrigerator on the counter to allow the dough to warm up for about 20 minutes.

At the same time, in a Dutch oven or large pot, bring 4 quarts of water and the remaining malt syrup to a boil over high heat.

(recipe continues through page 113)

Take one dough ball, and with both index fingers and thumbs, pinch the center of the dough, punching a hole in it (2). With the help of gravity, gently stretch and turn the dough ring (3) until the dough itself is about 1 inch thick and the ring measures 5 inches in diameter (4). Return it to the greased baking sheet and repeat with the remaining dough.

Working in batches, boil the dough rings in the malt water for 20 seconds per side, allowing the malt water to return to a boil between batches. Place the boiled dough rings on parchment-lined baking sheets.

Bake the bagels until they are golden brown, about 12 minutes. Allow the bagels to cool completely on a wire rack before serving.

The bagels will reach their height of fragrance only after cooling down completely, or ideally the next day. Stored in a brown paper bag or wrapped in plastic wrap, they will keep for up to 3 days on the counter; wrapped in plastic wrap, they will keep for up to 6 months in the freezer.

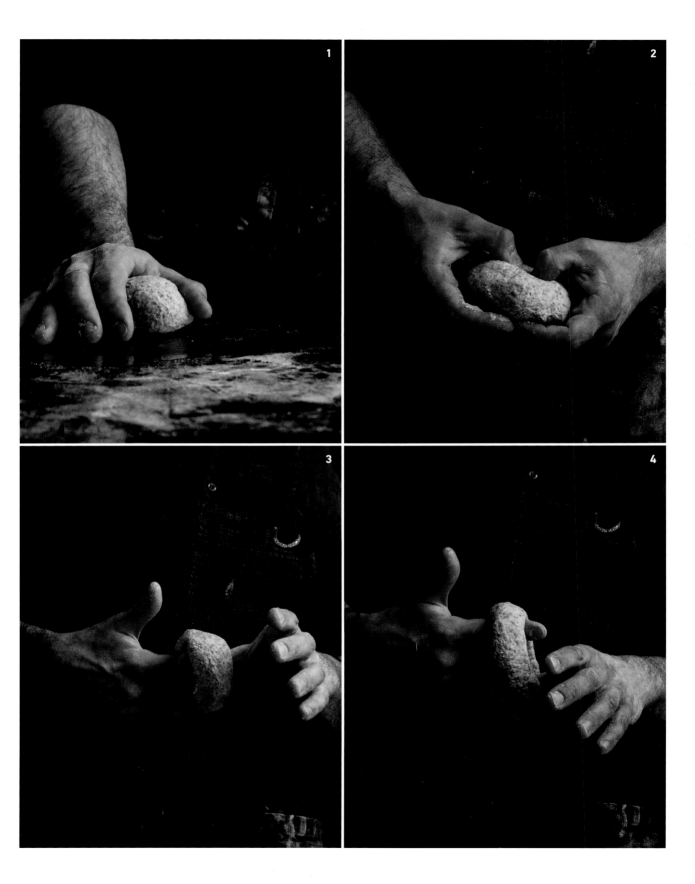

RYE BREAD

MAKES ONE 13 × 4-INCH LOAF

My high school friend Aileen Murphy spent a year in Germany baking with the great Herta Breuer. Aileen returned to the States with tons of handwritten recipes from Herta's bakery. I get kind of giddy looking over the recipes in the original German, with words like *Wasser* (water) and *Sauerteig* (sourdough) that are so close to the English that you can almost understand the whole thing. This is one of those recipes, and it is all about flavor and texture. For a lot of the bread in the world, including many of my recipes, the process is all about building and managing strength. When you work with rye, however, you can be gleefully free of these necessities. The grain has barely any gluten, so it is nearly impossible to build strength with a 100% rye dough. Strength isn't the objective with this ancient grain. Instead, it's all about the texture and flavor, which you tease out through fermentation. Milled rye has a really mild aroma, whereas fermenting rye raises its aroma volume to the max. In Germany, rye bread is sold the day after baking, allowing even more flavor to develop as it rests. Begin this dough 48 hours before you plan to bake it, and let the loaf rest overnight before slicing.

FOR THE PREFERMENT

500 grams water, warmed to 77°F

500 grams coarse cracked rye, soaked in water overnight and drained (recipe follows)

500 grams rye flour

50 grams rye levain (see page 90)

FOR THE BREAD DOUGH

500 grams rye flour

500 grams coarse cracked rye, soaked in water overnight and drained (recipe follows)

70 grams raw sunflower seeds

70 grams raw flaxseeds

30 grams raw linseeds

30 grams raw sesame seeds

30 grams sea salt

20 grams turbinado sugar, such as Sugar in the Raw

900 grams water, warmed to 77°F

Nonstick cooking spray

MAKE THE PREFERMENT: Combine the water, drained cracked rye, rye flour, and levain in a medium bowl. Cover the bowl with plastic wrap and set it aside to let the dough ferment at room temperature for 24 hours. There will be signs of fermentation, such as bubbles on the surface and around the edges of the mixture.

MAKE THE BREAD DOUGH: In a large bowl, combine the preferment, rye flour, cracked rye, sunflower seeds, flaxseeds, linseeds, sesame seeds, salt, sugar, and the water. Mix by hand until fully incorporated. Pour the dough into a Pullman loaf pan or metal bread pan that has been greased with nonstick cooking spray. Cover with the Pullman cover or aluminum foil and set it aside to ferment at room temperature for 4 hours. The dough will become very aromatic while fermenting.

Preheat the oven to 375°F.

Bake the loaf, covered, until it is firm and the crust has turned a silvery gray-brown, about 1 hour.

Set the loaf pan on a wire rack to cool for at least 4 hours, and ideally overnight, before slicing.

Stored in a brown paper bag or wrapped in plastic wrap, rye bread keeps well for up to 10 days on the counter; wrapped in plastic wrap, it will keep for up to 6 months in the freezer.

CRACKED RYE

1,000 grams rye

Run the rye through a mill on a setting that just breaks the grains apart and cuts them to a quarter of their size.

To prepare the cracked rye for this bread, place it in a container, cover it with 3 times its volume in water, and soak overnight. Drain before using.

REGULATING YOUR OVEN TEMPERATURE

A home oven's temperature can be really difficult to calibrate and temperature readings may be unreliable, so take that into consideration when baking and get to know the idiosyncrasies of your appliance. For added insurance, use an oven thermometer to make sure you get an accurate reading of your oven's internal temperature. In a professional kitchen, I can regulate the temperature of my oven precisely, and a professional oven can reach temperatures that far exceed those of a home oven. In a home setting, there are easy tricks for generating extra heat. I recommend preheating a Dutch oven in which to bake your bread loaves and covering that Dutch oven with a lid to create steam as the bread bakes. These steps will inhibit the Maillard reaction, a chemical process during which the surface of the bread browns and crust forms, and thereby allow the dough to continue to expand while it is baking. You'll also get a feeding frenzy of yeast as the baking temperature increases and these yeasts create gas, which gets trapped in the dough, resulting in an open crumb, just what we're after for yeasted and sourdough loaves.

MAKING PASTA

If you're a pasta novice, I want you to forget about recipes for a moment and instead get acquainted with how dough feels beneath your fingertips. A properly mixed pasta dough should have the consistency of Play-Doh and feel tacky but not sticky. Focus on how the mixture feels and how different flours behave when mixed with water and with one another.

Start with a cup of all-purpose flour from the supermarket: Place it on a work surface and make a well in the middle. Add ¾ cup water to the well and, using a fork, work in from the edges of the well to gradually incorporate the flour. The flour and water mixture will go from looking like clumps of cheese curd to forming a shaggy dough. The next time, do the same thing with Red Fife flour and see how a fresh-milled flour absorbs more water than all-purpose flour and how it feels beneath your fingers as it comes together. For the next try, mix Blue Beard durum with the water and notice how the durum dough feels slightly different from the one made with all-purpose or Red Fife.

For me, pasta making is all about feeling—and it's important to keep that in mind as you practice. When you have mastered the recipes and techniques with lots of repetition (remember, no one's grandma was a pasta master at birth), forget the recipes and "freestyle," allowing your flour and liquid quantities to be guided by how the dough feels. This will bring you closer to the spirit of Italian pasta making—and really, Italian cooking in general. My grandma and my mom both used to grab a bunch of ingredients and just mix them together. They may not have been precise with their measurements, but they knew exactly how the ingredients affected one another and how they were supposed to feel. They knew that if the dough was too wet, they added flour. If it was too dry, they added a little water until it was just right.

The recipes here include instructions for making adjustments based on the conditions of your kitchen and variations in ingredients so you get a pasta dough with the perfect consistency, no matter where you are, every time. I encourage you to trust your instincts, learn the proper feel of a dough, and play around with different flours and blends. Let the consistency and the strength of the dough inspire its final shape and its sauce.

CHOOSING THE RIGHT GRAIN FOR THE JOB

When it comes to choosing a grain for pasta, the characteristics of that grain combined with the choice of wet ingredients (water, egg yolk, or whole eggs) will determine the shape the dough can hold. There are literally thousands of pasta shapes—there are whole books dedicated to this vast topic—but I have chosen a few of the most common ones here, offering recipes for the doughs most adapted to those specific pasta forms.

For *pasta sfoglia*—sheets of pasta made with flour and egg yolks—the objective is to create a cooked pasta that has some bite, snap, and pliability to it. This pasta type favors hearty, protein-rich grains like hard red wheats. The egg yolk's fat lends pliability to the strong dough, allowing it to stretch, which is needed if you intend to roll the dough very thin for lasagna or to fill it to make ravioli.

Combining flour with whole eggs means the dough will have both the yolk's fat and the white's protein; this allows you to use a weaker flour with less protein, like soft spring wheat, and still have a strong and elastic dough. These conditions are ideal for noodles like tagliatelle, maltagliati, pappardelle, and tagliolini, which need to be thin, have bite, and hold together. Because an egg-heavy pasta has some protein from the whites and a larger quantity of fat from the yolk, it can be made with many different kinds of wheat and still hold its shape, but I like to use Sonora, a soft spring wheat.

For a flour-and-water dough, water populates the flour's starch and protein, which makes the starch swell and develops the gluten. All this happens in the absence of added fat or protein, so you need a very strong flour like durum. The absence of yolk fat means the dough cannot stretch very much without breaking, making it ideal for small, shorter pasta shapes like orecchiette and cavatelli.

As you become more comfortable using freshly milled flour to make pasta, you can begin blending flours in order to combine traits. I use wine as an analogy: If you have a really tannic grape with high alcohol and acidity, you can blend in a lighter grape to balance out those characteristics. Similarly, if you have a wheat with low protein, such as rye, you can cut it with one that brings more protein, like Kansas Turkey, and achieve shapes that ask for stronger flours.

As an advanced pasta maker, I love experimenting with flour mixes, so if I have some rye, some winter wheat, and some spring wheat hanging around—or any other combination, really—I will mix them together, see how the dough behaves, and then select the pasta shape accordingly. Remember, it's all about the feel. What's fun about making pasta from a creative flour mixture is that the results are immediate because the dough doesn't have to ferment. You can see and feel the dough immediately and, with experience, determine the shape it should take.

MILLING FOR PASTA

When milling flour to make pasta at home, the flour doesn't have to be as fine as bread flour. And it can be a bit coarser still for certain kinds of shapes, like cavatelli, where tradition and function favor semolina. Ravioli dough, on the other hand, requires a slightly finer grind.

EXTRACTION

You can make all of the pasta recipes here with 100% bran inclusion, but I recommend sifting out the bran, then adding a percentage back to taste. If you're stone-milling at home, there is always going to be some bran in your flour even if you sift it meticulously. But if you like the hearty, in-your-face aroma of the wheat you're using, don't sift the flour at all. I base how much I add back on the sauce I am using. If it's something strong like a concentrated, hearty Bolognese, I add 5% of the weight of the flour—for example,

I add 25 grams of bran to 500 grams of flour. For milder sauces like Alfredo, I sift out all the bran and rely on the bran that is naturally present due to stone-milling.

Bear in mind that bran takes on more water and that pastas made with bran can get crumbly if not adequately hydrated. Generally speaking, having a high bran content doesn't affect the flour or blend that you use, and bran is so thin that it is not an obstacle to rolling the dough very thin. It mainly influences the amount of water added.

MIXING AND KNEADING

When mixing pasta dough, your main objective is to hydrate the flour and allow the gluten to develop. After the dry and liquid ingredients are fully incorporated, knead the dough energetically to further develop the gluten, thereby strengthening the dough. No matter what flours you mix, once you have kneaded the dough, allow it to sit for 30 minutes, covered with a clean kitchen towel or plastic wrap. This set-aside time will let the flour fully hydrate and the gluten rest, but it isn't enough time for the dough to begin fermenting as it would with bread or pizza dough. If the dough develops a dry skin, just roll it out before using it. Thanks to freshly milled flour's oil-rich nature, the skin will be absorbed back into the dough with a few rolls of a rolling pin.

CONSERVING THE DOUGH

The raw, unshaped dough for tagliatelle, maltagliati, pappardelle, tagliolini, pici, tonnarelli, orecchiette, and cavatelli will keep, tightly wrapped in plastic wrap, for up to 1 week in the refrigerator. Wrapped in plastic wrap, the shaped pasta freezes for up to a week, but the raw, unrolled dough does not freeze well.

COOKING

Most of the pasta dough recipes here yield four to six servings per half kilogram of pasta. Traditionally, Italians eat in courses: the *primo* (usually pasta) followed by the *secondo* (meat or fish). If you plan to do the same, the pasta course should feed six. If you are treating it as your main dish, the recipe serves four.

Cook the pasta until al dente, meaning the pasta still has some firmness and bite to it. Taste the pasta as it cooks and cook until it is still a bit firm.

SAUCING

In Italy, cooks are very opinionated about which pasta shapes pair with which sauces. There's something of a science to it: long noodles go well with thick sauces and ragùs, while chunky sauces work best with shapes that "scoop" them up. The sauces in this chapter can, theoretically, be paired with any pasta, but I have recommended the ones that pair best, based on Italian sensibilities. I have also given some choices for ravioli fillings.

PASTA SFOGLIA DOUGH FOR LASAGNA AND RAVIOLI

MAKES ABOUT 750 GRAMS (1⅔ POUNDS) PASTA

Pasta sfoglia is a sheet of pasta that can be layered to make lasagna or filled to make ravioli. After years of developing my ideal *pasta sfoglia* recipe, I landed on this dough. It is perfectly pliable when cooked and has a satisfying bite. The farro flour is bold in flavor and highly distinctive, while the durum adds extensibility and a golden color. Meanwhile, the olive oil makes the dough soft and supple—ideal for lasagna as well as ravioli, both of which must be thin and flexible.

Ragù Bolognese (page 164) is the quintessential sauce for lasagna. For ravioli, use either filling on page 160 and your choice of sauce (pages 160–167).

VARIATIONS

- Replace the farro and durum with 400 grams Kansas Turkey wheat flour and 100 grams mesquite flour. The mesquite delivers nice flavor but takes away a bit of strength from the dough, which I can get away with because Kansas Turkey is a fantastically strong, protein-rich grain.

- Replace the farro and durum with 450 grams Kansas Turkey wheat flour and 50 grams freekeh. Freekeh is a green cereal made from a young durum. The berries are roasted, then rubbed in a process that destroys their nutritional value through friction. What it loses in nutrition it gains in flavor. Freekeh is weak but Kansas Turkey is there to provide nutrition and structure.

- Replace the farro and durum with 400 grams Kansas Turkey wheat flour and 100 grams rye flour. Because rye is very weak but has a lot of flavor, you compensate for its lack of strength by using Kansas Turkey.

350 grams farro flour

150 grams durum wheat flour (I like Blue Beard)

12 large egg yolks, beaten

14 grams (1 tablespoon) extra-virgin olive oil

Durum semolina, for dusting

Bench flour (see tip on page 138), for dusting

As an alternative to farro and durum—if, for example, you have only a weak flour, such as a soft spring wheat—you can build strength by laminating the dough: fold the pasta and pass it through a pasta machine a total of 25 times. Since you're folding and turning, you create strength through a sort of cross-hatching.

In a large bowl, whisk together the farro and durum flours. Pour the combined flours onto a work surface and make a well in the middle. Add the egg yolks and the olive oil and beat together with a fork. Working in from the edges of the well, continue using the fork to gradually incorporate the flour with the egg mixture to form a shaggy dough. The dough should feel tacky but not sticky. If the dough sticks to your fingers, add 1 tablespoon more flour. If the dough feels too dry, add water, a tablespoon at a time, until it reaches the desired consistency. Knead the dough energetically with both hands until it is a smooth, compact mass, 10 to 12 minutes. Wrap the dough in a semolina-dusted kitchen towel or plastic

wrap, and set it aside to rest at room temperature for about 30 minutes.

IF MAKING LASAGNA: With a knife, cut off a 150-gram (5-ounce) piece of dough, transfer it to a work surface lightly dusted with bench flour, and work it into a rough rectangle with a rolling pin: Working from the center to the edges, push forward and roll the dough out as thin as possible. You should get to about ⅛ inch of thickness before it starts pushing back. Turn the dough 180 degrees and repeat the forward pushing motion. Roll about 4 inches of the dough around the rolling pin, and roll it to a thickness you can see through. Continue for the entire length of the dough. Turn the dough 180 degrees and repeat

(recipe continues through page 127)

the rolling process once more. (The sheet should now measure about 8 × 20 inches.) Repeat with the remaining dough to make a total of 5 sheets.

Dust the dough with semolina and set aside on baking sheets. Wrapped in plastic wrap, the pasta will keep for up to 1 week in the freezer. Do not refrigerate it.

To make the lasagna, preheat the oven to 375°F. Lightly grease a baking sheet with extra-virgin olive oil.

Meanwhile, bring a large pot of water to a boil over high heat. Salt the water. When the salt has dissolved, add the pasta sheets and cook for 1 minute. Drain. Place a sheet of pasta on the oiled baking sheet, and spoon some ragù bolognese over it, distributing it evenly. Continue to layer the pasta and sauce until they are used up and a pasta sheet is the final layer. Bake until the pasta is cooked through and the edges are crispy and browned, about 25 minutes.

IF MAKING RAVIOLI: Follow the instructions for lasagna up to the point where you have a total of 5 sheets of dough.

Dust the dough with bench flour. Pipe or spoon tablespoons of the desired filling over half of the sheet (1), leaving a 3-inch border from the edges of the sheet and 3 inches between each portion of filling (2). Spray the half with the filling with a fine mist of water or moisten the dough by hand, and then fold the remaining dough over the filling to close (3). With your fingers, press gently around the filling, eliminating any air bubbles and ensuring the dough fits snugly around the filling and is pressed together around the edges of the filling (4). With a pasta wheel or knife, separate the ravioli, leaving an equal border around each raviolo. Or use a 2½-inch cookie cutter to separate the ravioli. Repeat with the remaining dough. You should have around thirty 2½-inch ravioli.

To cook the ravioli, bring a large pot of water to a boil over high heat. Salt the water. When the salt has dissolved, add the ravioli and cook until al dente, about 2 minutes. Drain and serve with your choice of sauce.

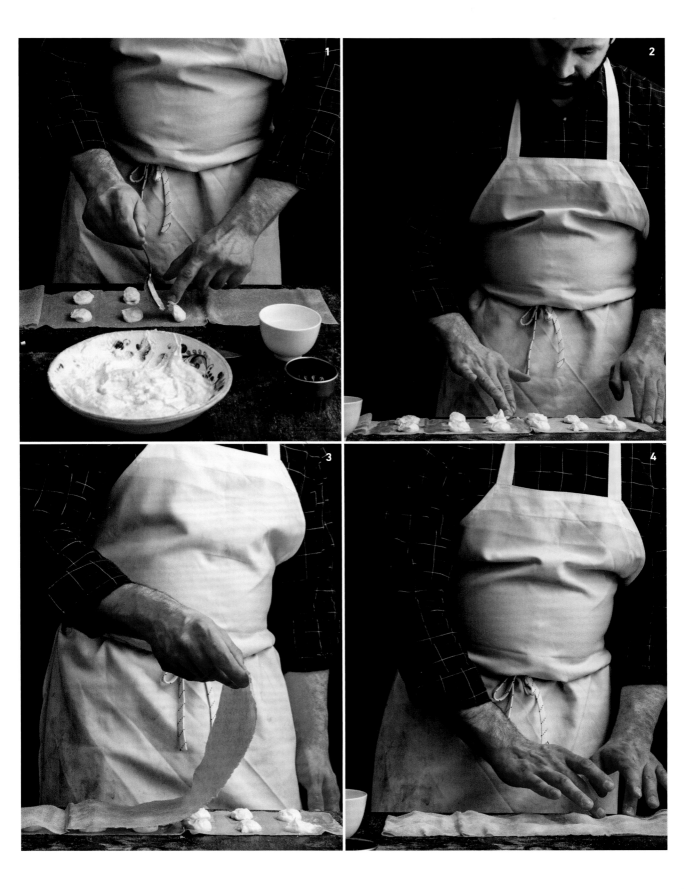

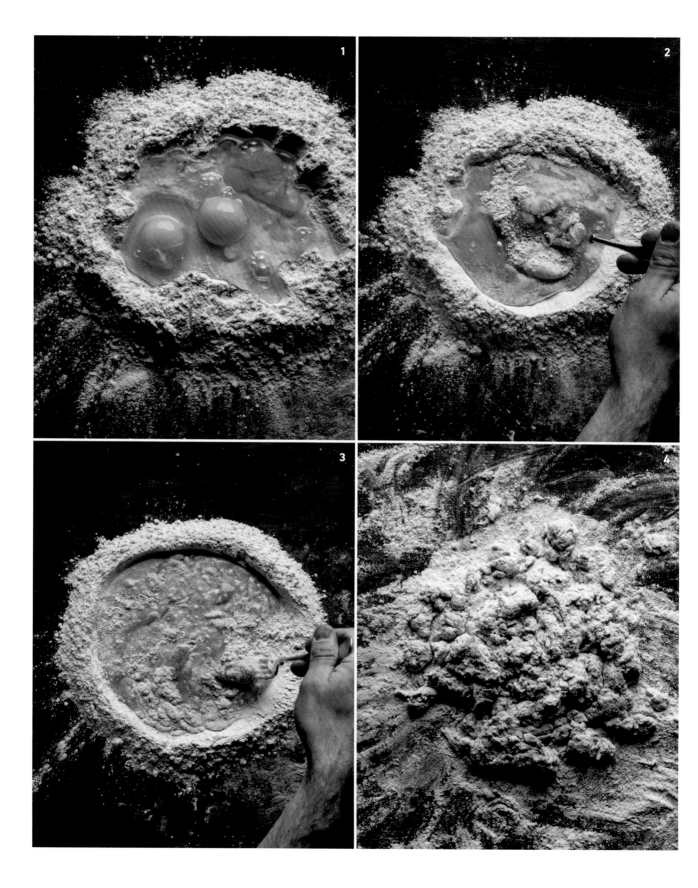

WHOLE-EGG DOUGH FOR TAGLIATELLE, MALTAGLIATI, PAPPARDELLE, AND TAGLIOLINI

MAKES ABOUT 800 GRAMS (1¾ POUNDS) PASTA

At Vetri we used one dough for all our fresh pastas, whether we were making ravioli, pappardelle, or fettuccine. We used only egg yolks. When I departed for Bergamo to work at Osteria della Brughiera, I figured I would find a similar yolk-rich approach to their dough, maybe applied to some highly regional pasta shape I had never seen. But when I arrived, what I saw blew my mind. They used freshly milled flour—remember, I didn't really know what that meant yet, but the flavor was incredible—and no two pasta recipes were identical. Of course now this makes total sense to me: each dough was adapted to its singular use. The chefs' use of whole eggs instead of just yolks also clicked for me because it resulted in zero waste, a mirror of how most Bergamaschi actually cook. A whole egg has more water than a yolk alone has, and it also has more protein. The protein from the egg white gives strength and helps to make an al dente noodle when combined with soft spring wheats like Frederick or Sonora, which aren't ideal for yolk-only noodles because of their low protein content. Shapes like tagliatelle, maltagliati, pappardelle, and tagliolini need the strength from this protein; otherwise the noodles will break.

VARIATIONS

- Replace the soft spring wheat flour with 375 grams Redeemer wheat flour and 125 grams einkorn flour. Einkorn has lots of flavor but little strength, so it works in perfect harmony with a strong and comparatively bland Redeemer flour.

- Combine 500 grams of soft spring wheat flour (I like Sonora) with 2 large eggs plus 4 egg yolks. This yolk-heavy variation uses whole eggs in combination with additional yolks to give the dough greater fat and richness. The egg whites provide the protein the soft spring wheat needs in order to give the noodle a bit of a bite.

500 grams soft spring wheat flour (I like Frederick or Sonora)

5 large eggs, beaten

Durum semolina, for dusting

Bench flour (see tip on page 138), for dusting

Whether you are making tagliatelle, maltagliati, pappardelle, or tagliolini, you can "cheat" the kneading phase by passing the shaggy dough through a pasta machine instead of doing it by hand. This will cut the kneading time to about 2 minutes.

Pour the flour onto a work surface and make a well in the middle. Add the eggs (1) and beat them with a fork (2). Working in from the edges of the well, continue using the fork to gradually incorporate the flour with the eggs (3) to form a shaggy dough (4). The dough should feel tacky but not sticky. If the dough sticks to your fingers, add 1 tablespoon more flour. If the dough feels too dry, add water, a tablespoon at a time, until it reaches the desired consistency. Knead the dough energetically with both hands until it is a smooth, compact mass, 10 to 12 minutes. Wrap the dough in a semolina-dusted kitchen towel or plastic wrap and set it aside to rest at room temperature for about 30 minutes.

(recipe continues through page 137)

IF MAKING TAGLIATELLE: With a bench scraper or knife, cut off a 150-gram (5-ounce) piece of dough (1), transfer it to a work surface lightly dusted with bench flour, and work it into a rough rectangle with a rolling pin (2): Working from the center to the edges, push forward and roll the dough out as thin as possible. You should get to about ⅛ inch of thickness before it starts pushing back. Turn the dough 180 degrees and repeat the forward pushing motion. Roll about 4 inches of the dough around the rolling pin (3), and roll it to a thickness you can see through. Continue for the entire length of the dough. Turn the dough 180 degrees and repeat the rolling process once more. The sheet should measure about 8 × 20 inches (4). Repeat with the remaining dough.

Dust each piece of dough with bench flour, placing one layer over another. With one short edge facing you, fold about 2 inches of the near end of the dough over itself. Continue folding the dough over itself to form a loose, rectangular tube (5). Using a sharp knife, slice the dough into ¼-inch-wide strands (6). Pick up the dough strands and toss gently to separate them. Dust them with semolina and set them aside on a plate. Wrapped in plastic wrap, the pasta will keep for up to 1 week in the freezer. Do not refrigerate it.

To cook the tagliatelle, bring a large pot of water to a boil over high heat. Salt the water. When the salt has dissolved, add the tagliatelle and cook until al dente, about 30 seconds. Drain and serve with your choice of sauce (see pages 160–167).

IF MAKING MALTAGLIATI: Follow the procedure for tagliatelle until you dust each piece of dough with bench flour. Slice the dough diagonally into 2-inch-wide strips (7). Then cut each strip into diamonds measuring about 2 inches per side (8).

IF MAKING PAPPARDELLE: Follow the procedure for tagliatelle but cut the dough to a width of 1 inch (9).

IF MAKING TAGLIOLINI: Follow the procedure for tagliatelle but cut the dough to a width of ⅛ inch (10).

PAPPARDELLE

TAGLIOLINI

MALTAGLIATI

TAGLIATELLE

FLOUR-AND-WATER DOUGH FOR PICI AND TONNARELLI

MAKES 775 GRAMS (ABOUT 1⅔ POUNDS) PASTA

The first time I visited Tuscany, Marc Vetri took me to meet *Signora Dania Lucherini* at La Chiusa, a hotel and restaurant in a beautifully restored farmhouse in Montefollonico. Dania had been making pasta there for twenty years and to her, our countless questions about pasta shapes and tools must have seemed overzealous. For Signora Dania, novel shapes were not nearly as important as the flour that she used: a rustic blend milled down the street. We spent some time watching her work. She was the first person I ever saw use coarse stone-milled Tipo 1 flour instead of a roller-milled Tipo 00 for pappardelle. She didn't use eggs in her pasta at all; she said they were for the upper class and the tradition of pasta where she is from was less extravagant, meant for average people. Meanwhile back in Philly, I had been struggling to get forty egg yolks into a kilo of semolina. The experience was eye-opening.

The best dish of our stay was a simple bowl of pici, the classic Tuscan noodle, which is rolled by hand and served with potent sauces like game ragù. I still remember the taste of the pasta itself, flavored strongly by freshly milled flour. I was eager to re-create the texture and flavor of Signora Dania's pici. I imagined she used a high-protein, highly flavorful flour. My choice was Kansas Turkey wheat. And I marry the pici with a condiment of fragrant garlic, floral olive oil, and subtly piquant pepper without it being overpowered by—or overpowering—these flavors. The result is pure harmony.

I use pici dough to make tonnarelli, as well. Also known as *spaghetti alla chitarra* because in some regions the pasta is made by rolling the dough over an instrument featuring wires that resemble guitar strings, tonnarelli are long strands of squared-off spaghetti. Protein-rich hard winter wheat gives just the bite and structure I am looking for in such a pasta strand.

VARIATIONS

- Replace hard winter wheat flour with 450 grams Red Fife flour and 50 grams Red Russian flour. Strong Red Fife mixed with extensible, stretchy Red Russian flour combines to create a noodle with a pleasing bite.

- Replace hard winter wheat flour with 400 grams Blue Beard durum semolina and 100 grams Sonora soft spring wheat flour. The very strong and extensible durum conspires with the delicate and soft Sonora flour to make a suitable variation that has a pleasing bite and an interesting flavor.

---

500 grams hard winter wheat flour (I like Kansas Turkey)

275 grams tepid water

Durum semolina or bench flour (see tip), for dusting

Extra-virgin olive oil, for pici

When you dust a work surface to make pasta or to shape bread, use a bench scraper to gather any excess flour and store it in a sealed container in a cool, dry place. Use the recycled flour in recipes calling for "bench flour." This is a practical way to incorporate unused flour, reducing waste.

Pour the flour onto a work surface and make a well in the middle. Add about a third of the water (1). Working in from the edges of the well, use a fork to incorporate a bit of the flour with the water (2). Continue to add the water in thirds, gradually incorporating the flour to

(recipe continues through page 145)

form a shaggy dough (3). The dough should feel tacky but not sticky. If the dough sticks to your fingers, add 2 tablespoons more flour. If the dough feels too dry, add water, a teaspoon at a time, until it reaches the desired consistency. Knead the dough energetically with both hands until it is a smooth, compact mass, 10 to 12 minutes (4). Wrap the dough in a semolina-dusted kitchen towel or plastic wrap and set it aside to rest at room temperature for about 30 minutes.

IF MAKING PICI: With a knife, cut off a 150-gram (5-ounce) piece of dough, transfer it to a work surface lightly dusted with bench flour, and work it into a rough rectangle with a rolling pin: Working from the center to the edges, push forward and roll the dough out as thin as possible. You should get to about ⅛ inch of thickness before it starts pushing back. Turn the dough 180 degrees and repeat the forward pushing motion. (The sheet should measure about 8 × 20 inches.)

Dip one hand in olive oil and rub a thin sheen of oil over the entire surface of the dough. Repeat with the remaining dough. Set it aside to rest for about 30 minutes.

With a knife, cut the dough lengthwise into 1-inch-wide strips.

Roll each strip lengthwise into a long, tight tube: Pressing one end of the dough onto your work surface, use your other hand to roll the dough to a thickness of about ⅛ inch. Coil up the pici, dust with semolina, and set aside on a plate. Wrapped in plastic wrap, the pasta will keep for up to 1 week in the freezer. Do not refrigerate it.

To cook the pici, bring a large pot of water to a boil over high heat. Salt the water. When the salt has dissolved, add the pici and cook until al dente, about 3 minutes. Drain and serve with your choice of sauce (see pages 160–167).

IF MAKING TONNARELLI: With a knife, cut off a 150-gram (5-ounce) piece of dough, transfer it to a work surface lightly dusted with bench flour, and work it into a rough rectangle with a rolling pin: Working from the center to the edges, push forward and roll it out to about $\frac{1}{16}$ inch of thickness. If necessary, turn the dough 180 degrees and repeat the forward pushing motion. (The sheet should measure about 8 × 20 inches.) Repeat with the remaining dough.

Dust each sheet of dough with bench flour (see the tip on page 138), placing one layer over another. With one short edge facing you, fold about 2 inches of the far end of the dough over itself. Continue folding the dough over itself to form a loose, rectangular tube. Using a sharp knife, slice the dough into $\frac{1}{16}$-inch-thick strands. Pick up the dough strands and toss gently to separate them. Dust the tonnarelli with semolina and set them aside on a plate. Wrapped in plastic wrap, the pasta will keep for up to 1 week in the freezer. Do not refrigerate it.

To cook the tonnarelli, bring a large pot of water to a boil over high heat. Salt the water. When the salt has dissolved, add the tonnarelli and cook until al dente, about 3 minutes. Drain and serve with your choice of sauce (see pages 160–167).

ITALIAN FLOUR GRADES

Italian and American mills do not categorize flours the same way. In Italy flours milled from soft wheat are labeled "grano tenero," which is the most common grade, and are used to make bread, pasta, pizza, and pastry. Flours milled from hard wheats are labeled "semola" or "grano duro." The American analogue is semolina, which in both countries is rather granular compared with other flour grades and has a yellowish tint. Semolina is used to make pasta and bread.

Flours in Italy are milled to various fineness and bran inclusions. Tipo 00, also known as "Doppio 0" flour, is white and powdery with the lowest bran inclusion and can be milled from either soft or hard wheats. Its protein content, therefore, ranges significantly, from 7% to 11%. Tipo 0 has a bit more bran inclusion than 00 and is similar in strength to American all-purpose flour. Tipo 1 is less fine and has more bran (around 80% bran inclusion) than Tipo 0, while Tipo 2 is less fine than Tipo 0 and has only around 10% of its bran removed. "Farina integrale" is whole wheat flour.

TONNARELLI

PICI

FLOUR-AND-WATER DOUGH FOR ORECCHIETTE AND CAVATELLI

MAKES ABOUT 1,000 GRAMS (2¼ POUNDS) PASTA

The orecchiette and cavatelli shapes come from Italy's deep south, the area that straddles the regions of Puglia and Basilicata where the Murgia Plateau rises up from the Adriatic Sea. There, durum wheat fields supply local mills with grain for bread and pasta. When it comes to hand-shaped durum wheat pasta, tradition calls for a coarse grind called semolina (see page 31). Semolina is one of those words that gets a bit mixed up in translation. It's not a grain, but rather the term that describes coarsely ground durum wheat, per the Italian tradition. When milling, a coarser grind gives a bigger yield, which is likely why it is so ubiquitous in southern Italy, where frugal practices reign. Locals there listened to their pasta doughs and developed forms best adapted to durum's high gluten potential but low extensibility. The result was short, thick pasta shapes like orecchiette and cavatelli.

500 grams durum wheat semolina (I like Blue Beard), plus more for dusting

125 grams soft spring wheat flour (I like Sonora)

9 grams sea salt

385 grams water, warmed to 65°F

In a large bowl, whisk together the durum and soft spring wheat flours and the salt. Pour the mixture onto a work surface and make a well in the middle. Add half of the water and mix by hand, working from the edges of the well into the center. Add the remaining water a little at a time, gradually incorporating the flour to form a shaggy dough. The dough should feel tacky but not sticky. If the dough sticks to your fingers, add 2 tablespoons more flour. If the dough feels too dry, add water, a teaspoon at a time, until it reaches the desired consistency. Knead the dough energetically with both hands until it is a smooth, compact mass, 10 to 12 minutes. Wrap the dough in a semolina-dusted kitchen towel or plastic wrap and set it aside to rest at room temperature for about 30 minutes.

IF MAKING ORECCHIETTE: Flatten the dough into a disk about ½ inch thick on a work surface lightly dusted with semolina. Cut off a strip of dough about ½ inch wide. Pressing down on the dough with your fingertips, roll the dough back and forth to form a long strand about ¼ inch thick (1). Cut the strand into ½-inch pieces (2). With a knife pressed into the edge of one piece, drag the dough across the work surface, forming a roughly circular curled-up pasta shape (3). Invert the pasta shape so the rough part faces outward (4). Dust it with semolina and set it aside on a plate. Repeat with the remaining dough. Wrapped in plastic wrap, the pasta will keep for up to 1 week in the freezer. Do not refrigerate it.

To cook the orecchiette, bring a large pot of water to a boil over high heat. Salt the water. When the salt has dissolved, add the orecchiette and cook until al dente, about 3 minutes. Drain and serve with your choice of sauce (see pages 160–167).

(recipe continues through page 149)

IF MAKING CAVATELLI: Flatten the dough into a disk about ½ inch thick on a work surface lightly dusted with semolina. Cut off a strip of dough about ½ inch wide. Pressing down on the dough with your fingertips, roll the dough back and forth to form a long strand about ½ inch thick. Cut the strand into ½-inch pieces. With your thumb, press each pasta piece into the tines of an inverted fork to form a ridged and curled pasta shape (5, 6). Dust them with semolina and set them aside on a plate. Repeat with the remaining dough. Wrapped in plastic wrap, the pasta will keep for up to 1 week in the freezer. Do not refrigerate it.

To cook the cavatelli, bring a large pot of water to a boil over high heat. Salt the water. When the salt has dissolved, add the cavatelli and cook until al dente, about 3 minutes. Drain and serve with your choice of sauce (see pages 160–167).

POTATO GNOCCHI DOUGH

SERVES 6 TO 8

Potato gnocchi are a central Italian pasta and they are especially typical of Rome, where they are served at trattorias and homes on Thursdays in order to fill up bellies before the lean Friday meals prescribed by the Catholic calendar. I make my gnocchi the way I make biscuits: with a bench scraper to cut all the ingredients together. Doing so makes the texture light and fluffy, which achieves that pillowy consistency ideal in potato gnocchi. The rye flour gives the dough flavor but has very little gluten, which also guarantees the dough's lightness. This is one of the few recipes in which I include US cups for measuring flour because you don't need metric precision here and the amount of flour you need will actually vary somewhat depending on your potatoes. Through trial and error, I have found that using half waxy and half starchy potatoes creates gnocchi with a delightful mouthfeel. Choose potatoes that are all about the same size so they cook evenly in the same amount of time.

900 grams (about 2 pounds) potatoes (I use half Idaho and half Yukon Gold)

250 grams (2½ cups) rye flour, plus more for dusting

3 eggs, beaten

175 g (1½ cups) finely grated Parmigiano-Reggiano

25 grams (1½ tablespoons) sea salt

Semolina (see page 31), for dusting

Place the potatoes in a medium pot and cover with cold water. Salt the water and bring to a boil over medium-low heat. Cook until the potatoes are fork-tender, 40 minutes to 1 hour.

Drain the potatoes and peel them while they are still hot. Pass the potatoes through a ricer, and then press them directly onto a work surface. Distribute 2 cups of the flour, eggs and cheese (1, 2, 3) evenly over the potatoes and season with the salt. With a bench scraper, cut the ingredients just until they come together (4). If the dough seems too wet, add the remaining flour, 2 tablespoons at a time. (You may not need all the flour.) Knead the dough with your hands until the flour and egg are incorporated, about 15 seconds (5).

With a bench scraper, cut off a 150-gram (5-ounce) piece of dough (6), keeping the remaining dough covered with a clean kitchen towel. Working from the center outward on a surface lightly dusted with rye flour, roll the dough to form a 1½-inch-thick cord (7); then cut the cord into equal bite-size pieces (8). Dust them with semolina and set them aside on a platter. Repeat with the remaining dough. The gnocchi will keep, uncovered, for 2 days in the refrigerator or, wrapped in plastic wrap, for up to a month in the freezer.

To cook the gnocchi, bring a large pot of water to a boil over high heat. Salt the water. When the salt has dissolved, add the gnocchi in batches and cook until they float, about 3 minutes. Drain and set them aside on a plate. Serve with your choice of sauce (see pages 160–167).

(recipe continues through page 155)

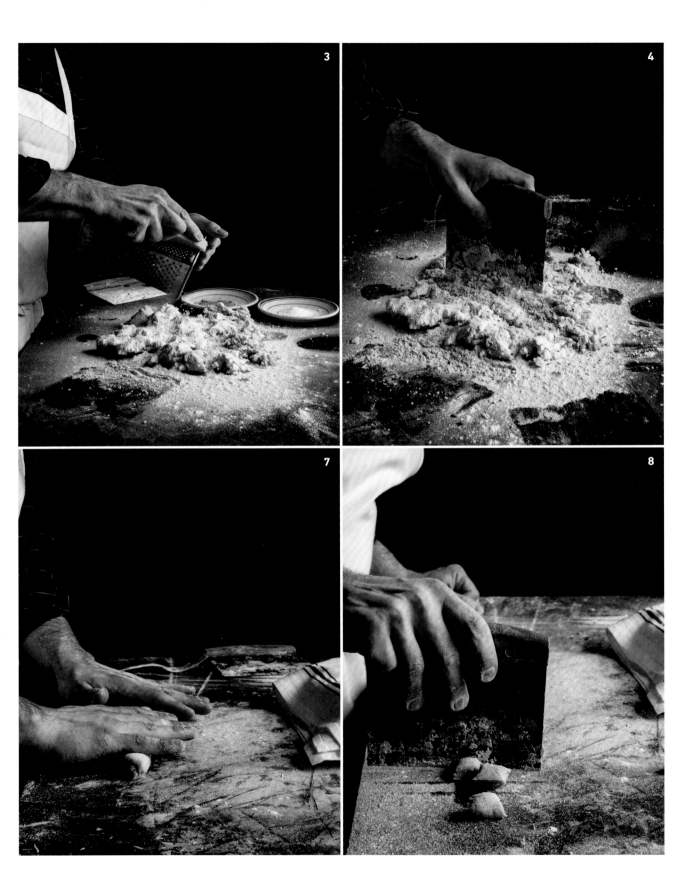

CANEDERLI

SERVES 4 TO 6

Although many people are familiar with bread dumplings by way of German and Austrian cuisine, I first encountered them in northern Italy, where they are called canederli and are the signature dish of the northeastern region of Südtirol (Alto Adige). Dishes from this German-speaking part of Italy share more with those of neighboring Austria than with their Italian counterparts to the south. There are as many canederli recipes as there are cooks and they might contain liver, speck, or even dried fruits. Their purpose, aside from being delicious and sustaining, is to give stale bread a second life. I used to soak the bread in stock, milk, or even beet juice, but now I just use water because my recipe has plenty of its own flavor from the freshly milled flour. To make this a heartier meal, I like to wilt some Swiss chard in the broth and top the whole dish with a poached egg.

500 grams week-old bread (I like the Yeasted Loaf, page 71), crusts separated and torn, crumb cut into 1-inch cubes

150 grams unsalted butter, softened

120 grams spelt flour

5 large eggs, beaten

75 grams finely grated Grana Padano

1 bunch fresh parsley, finely chopped

½ teaspoon grated nutmeg

Sea salt

2,000 grams (about 2 quarts) chicken stock

If the canederli mixture is sticky, wet your hands with warm water before rolling it.

Place the cubed bread in a colander, rinse it lightly with warm water, and set aside. The bread should be moistened but not sopping wet. Squeeze out any excess liquid.

Pulse the bread crusts in a food processor until ground to the size of coarse coffee grounds.

In a large bowl, combine the moistened bread cubes, the ground bread crusts, the butter, flour, eggs, Grana Padano, parsley, nutmeg, and salt to taste. Mix thoroughly by hand. Form the mixture into balls roughly the size of golf balls.

In a 4-quart pot, bring the stock to a boil over high heat. Salt the stock. When the salt has dissolved, add the canederli and simmer until cooked through, about 3 minutes. Serve immediately with the cooking stock.

PASSATELLI

SERVES 6 TO 8

In Italy there are two main types of pasta: fresh and dried. Fresh pasta, like lasagna or pici, is cooked while the dough is still tacky. Dried pasta, like rigatoni or ziti, is extruded and then essentially dehydrated for future use. As with all things Italian, there are exceptions to the rule. Passatelli is a fresh pasta that is also extruded: the dough for these bread-based noodles is forced through a potato ricer directly into boiling stock. I use sourdough bread here to bring some acidity as a foil to the rich, cheese-laden dough, and I prefer to use bread made from a flour with high gluten potential and high protein content so the pasta comes out like a compact noodle and not a soft, loose string.

250 grams sourdough bread (or ¼ Sourdough Loaf, page 81), crusts removed and discarded, crumb cut into 1-inch cubes

350 grams finely grated Parmigiano-Reggiano

300 grams hard wheat flour (I like Red Fife)

12 large eggs, beaten

½ teaspoon grated nutmeg

Sea salt

1,000 grams (1 quart) chicken stock

1 tablespoon coarsely chopped parsley

To expedite the bread drying process, preheat the oven to 250°F. Spread the bread cubes on a rimmed baking sheet and bake until crispy and completely dried out, 15 to 20 minutes.

Spread the bread cubes out on a rimmed baking sheet and set it aside, uncovered, overnight.

Transfer the bread cubes to a food processor and pulse until ground to the size of coarse coffee grounds. In a large bowl, combine the bread crumbs with the Parmigiano-Reggiano, flour, eggs, nutmeg, and salt to taste. Mix thoroughly by hand until the dough becomes creamy. Set it aside.

In a 2-quart pot, bring the stock to a boil over high heat. Salt the broth. When the salt has dissolved, working in batches, pass the dough through a potato ricer directly into the boiling stock. Cook until the passatelli float, about 3 minutes. Serve immediately with the cooking stock and chopped parsley sprinkled on top.

RAVIOLI FILLINGS

RICOTTA AND NUTMEG
SERVES 4 TO 6

400 grams (15 ounces) ricotta
(I like sheep's milk)

2 large eggs

Generous grating fresh nutmeg

Sea salt

In a medium bowl, mix together the ricotta, eggs, nutmeg, and salt to taste.

RICOTTA AND LEMON ZEST
SERVES 4 TO 6

400 grams (15 ounces) ricotta
(I like sheep's milk)

2 large eggs

Grated zest of 2 lemons

Sea salt

In a medium bowl, mix together the ricotta, eggs, lemon zest, and salt to taste.

PASTA SAUCES

BEET BUTTER
SERVES 4 TO 6

Best with ravioli, tagliatelle, maltagliati, pappardelle, tagliolini, pici, tonnarelli, and gnocchi.

2 medium beets

500 grams (about 1 pound) unsalted butter

20 sprigs fresh thyme

1 cup boiling water

Put the beets in a small saucepan, cover with water, and bring to a boil over high heat. Reduce the heat to a simmer, then cook until tender, about 1½ hours. Drain and set aside to cool.

Peel the beets, discarding the skins. In a medium bowl, mash the beets to a pulp with a fork.

In a large saucepan set over medium heat, combine the beets, butter, thyme, and the boiling water. Bring to a simmer, reduce the heat to low, and simmer until the liquid has reduced to the consistency of heavy cream, 3 to 4 minutes. Add the drained cooked pasta to the pan and mix gently to coat. Serve immediately.

Before you drain cooked pasta, always reserve a cup or more of the cooking water. The starchy water helps bind a sauce so it clings well to the pasta.

CHICKEN LIVER AND SAFFRON RAGÙ

SERVES 4 TO 6

Best with tagliatelle, maltagliati, and pappardelle.

Sea salt

7 chicken livers, halved

150 grams (½ cup plus 2 tablespoons) unsalted butter

¼ small white onion, sliced

Generous pinch saffron threads

½ cup boiling water

Salt the chicken livers as you would a steak and set aside. Heat 15 grams (1 tablespoon) of the butter and the onions in a large saucepan over medium heat. Salt the onions and cook until they are browned, about 10 minutes. Add the saffron and cook until fragrant, about 30 seconds. Add the boiling water and the remaining butter, and stir until melted.

Meanwhile, cook the pasta for 30 seconds, then add it to the pan with a few tablespoons of pasta cooking water. Stir gently, and then after about a minute, add the chicken livers. Swirl the pan and cook until the livers are just cooked through, about 1 minute. Serve immediately.

BROWN BUTTER

SERVES 4 TO 6

Best with gnocchi.

120 grams (8½ tablespoons) unsalted butter

Sea salt

30 grams (¼ cup) finely grated Parmigiano-Reggiano

Heat the butter in a medium skillet over medium heat until it has browned, 6 to 8 minutes. Remove the skillet from the heat, add the drained cooked pasta to the skillet, and swirl gently to coat. Season with salt to taste.

Serve immediately, sprinkling each portion with some Parmigiano-Reggiano.

PANCETTA RAGÙ

SERVES 4 TO 6

Best with ravioli, tagliatelle, tagliolini, pici, and tonnarelli.

15 grams (1 tablespoon) extra-virgin olive oil

1 small white onion, minced

Sea salt

85 grams (3 ounces) pancetta, cut into ¼-inch cubes

140 grams (5 ounces) sweet pork sausage, casings removed, chopped

90 grams (¾ cup) finely grated Parmigiano-Reggiano

Heat the olive oil in a large skillet over low heat. When the oil begins to shimmer, add the onion, season with salt, and cook until translucent, about 5 minutes. Add the pancetta and sausage and cook, stirring, until the sausage is cooked through, about 10 minutes.

Add the drained cooked pasta to the sauce in the skillet. Stir to coat. Remove the skillet from the heat, add ½ cup of the Parmigiano-Reggiano, and mix well. Season with salt to taste.

Serve immediately, sprinkling each portion with some of the remaining Parmigiano-Reggiano.

RAGÙ BOLOGNESE
SERVES 4 TO 6

Best with lasagna, tagliatelle, maltagliati, pappardelle, and tagliolini.

90 grams (¼ cup plus 2 tablespoons) extra-virgin olive oil

200 grams (7 ounces) ground beef

200 grams (7 ounces) ground pork

200 grams (7 ounces) ground veal

200 grams (7 ounces) ground pancetta

2 cups minced red onion

2 cups minced carrot

2 cups minced celery

Kosher salt

Freshly ground black pepper

2 garlic cloves, minced

1 cup red wine

2 (28-ounce) cans whole peeled San Marzano tomatoes, drained and crushed by hand

1 cup whole milk

340 grams (12 ounces) Parmigiano-Reggiano, rind and cheese separated, cheese grated, rind reserved

Pinch grated nutmeg

Preheat the oven to 300°F.

Heat the olive oil in a large ovenproof pot or Dutch oven over medium-high heat. When the oil begins to shimmer, add the beef, pork, veal, and pancetta. Stir constantly until browned, 3 to 4 minutes. Add the onion, carrot, and celery. Season with salt and black pepper to taste and cook, stirring constantly and scraping up any browned bits that stick to the bottom, until the vegetables caramelize, 2 to 3 minutes. Add the garlic and cook until soft, 7 to 8 minutes. Add the red wine, scraping up any browned bits. Cook until most of the liquid has been absorbed, about 2 minutes. Add the tomatoes, milk, and reserved Parmigiano-Reggiano rind.

Bring the sauce to a simmer and then transfer the pot to the oven. Cook, covered, for 45 minutes. Raise the heat to 375°F, uncover the pot, and cook for 10 minutes more.

Stir in the grated Parmigiano-Reggiano and the nutmeg. Adjust the salt and pepper to taste, and serve the ragù spooned over your choice of pasta.

RED PEPPER RAGÙ
SERVES 4 TO 6

Best with orecchiette and cavatelli.

90 grams (¼ cup plus 2 tablespoons) extra-virgin olive oil

2 garlic cloves, smashed

Florets from 1 bunch broccoli rabe

4 red bell peppers, roasted, peeled, and cut into ½-inch pieces

Ladle of boiling water

Sea salt

2 tablespoons chopped chives

25 grams (¼ cup) fine dried bread crumbs

Heat the olive oil in a large skillet over low heat. When the oil begins to shimmer, add the garlic and cook until it turns golden, about 5 minutes. Add the broccoli rabe, red peppers, the boiling water, and salt to taste. Raise the heat to high and simmer for 3 minutes.

Add the drained cooked pasta to the pan, stir to coat, and serve immediately with the chives and bread crumbs sprinkled on top.

CACIO E PEPE
SERVES 4 TO 6

Best with pappardelle, tonnarelli, and gnocchi.

180 grams (1½ cups) finely grated Pecorino Romano

60 grams (½ cup) finely grated Parmigiano-Reggiano

2 teaspoons freshly ground black pepper, plus more to taste

Ladle of boiling water

In a large bowl, combine 1 cup of the Pecorino Romano, the Parmigiano-Reggiano, and the pepper. Stir in the boiling water, and using the back of a large wooden spoon, mix vigorously and quickly to form a paste.

When the pasta is cooked, use a large strainer to remove it from the cooking water and quickly add it to the sauce in the bowl, keeping the cooking water boiling on the stove. Toss vigorously, adding more hot cooking water, a tablespoon or two at a time, as necessary to melt the cheese and to create a juicy sauce that completely coats the pasta.

Serve immediately, sprinkling each portion with the remaining Pecorino Romano and pepper to taste.

GARLIC, OIL, AND CHILE
SERVES 4 TO 6

Goes best with pici and tonnarelli.

70 grams (⅓ cup) extra-virgin olive oil

2 garlic cloves, smashed

1 fresh whole Thai bird chile or 1 teaspoon red pepper flakes

1 cup boiling water, or more as needed

1 cup fresh parsley, chopped

Juice of ¼ lemon

Heat the olive oil in a large skillet over low heat. When the oil begins to shimmer, add the garlic and cook until it turns golden, about 5 minutes. Add the chile and cook until fragrant, about 30 seconds.

Add the boiling water to the skillet, raise the heat to medium, and bring to a simmer, adding more water if the pan looks dry.

Add the drained cooked pasta to the skillet and stir well to coat. If the sauce is too dry, add a bit of cooking water and toss well. Remove from the heat, and stir in the parsley and lemon juice. Serve immediately.

MAKING
PIZZA

Pasta is my favorite food, but I see pizza as more life-sustaining. Not only is pizza a fermented product, making it theoretically healthy, but pasta is part of a meal while pizza *is* the meal. Pizza is also among the planet's most versatile foods since its definition is so malleable; in my view, it is any flatbread with toppings. You can really cast a wide net and find regional variations of pizza all around the world, but I'm focusing here on styles from the countries I am most familiar with: the United States and Italy.

CHOOSING THE RIGHT GRAIN FOR THE JOB

Chris Bianco, pizza-making legend and owner of Pizzeria Bianco and Tratto in Phoenix, Arizona, once told me that pizza is bread. He's right, of course, so when I think about pizza I apply bread-baking reasoning to choose the ideal flour. Considering pizza as a thin bread that has to stretch, I almost always reach for a flour that offers good extensibility (see page 31). You can let the dough ferment for a long time and let the acidity really run wild because the toppings can balance out the sour flavor.

Generally, my pizza recipes call for hard winter wheats, which provide strength and structure. But I am not limited to those varieties and often choose a blend of flours to impart flavor. Detroit-Style Pizza (page 190), for example, leans on Kansas Turkey wheat for strength and incorporates weak rye for its sweet flavor. When I need a dough to be stretchy and extensible, as for Pizza al Taglio (page 175) or Focaccia (page 194), I choose durum wheat blended with another flour to give strength, because durum on its own would disintegrate during the long fermentations those doughs undergo.

MILLING FOR PIZZA

Milling for pizza is similar to milling for bread (see page 67), except that you want to mill the flour slightly finer and extract a percentage of the bran (see page 30).

EXTRACTION

The razor-blade-like nature of bran interferes with the extensibility potential of pizza dough, so unless otherwise noted, extract 70% of the bran (30% inclusion) with a #70 mesh sieve (see page 30). Reserve the bran to use in other recipes.

If you want to try the advanced technique of making pizza dough with whole wheat flour, start with the focaccia recipe (page 194) and then work your way to the other pizza doughs, adding bran in 10% increments each time.

MIXING AND KNEADING

Some of the doughs begin with an autolyze phase (see page 31). This bread-making technique combines water and flour alone, allowing the water to hydrate the flour and to activate its enzymes naturally before the other ingredients are introduced. It works well for doughs that ferment for a short time, whereas long-fermented doughs don't benefit from the autolyze process. Almost all of the doughs are mixed in a stand mixer for a few minutes. The mixer simulates hand kneading and builds strength in the dough with minimal effort.

FERMENTING

Many of the doughs in this chapter have a long fermentation, some reaching 72 hours. With extended fermentation, there's a period in which strength increases but extensibility is diminished. But when the dough reaches a certain window, the dough's extensibility improves as the strength diminishes. You want to catch the dough at the sweet spot when it is still strong enough to capture air yet still fully extensible, resulting in a thin, crispy crust. With cold fermentation, you get a 4-hour window to find the sweet spot when the dough is perfectly fermented; room-temperature-fermented doughs, on the other hand, offer a much smaller margin of error. These recipes are designed for you to catch the dough at the right moment.

SHAPING

Some of the doughs are shaped on a water-dampened surface rather than a floured one. This technique provides the benefit of not introducing unfermented flour into the dough. It's easier to work with very hydrated doughs on water, but you do have to work more quickly to prevent the dough from becoming sticky.

STRETCHING

Stretching is the most deceptively challenging part of pizza making. It's a set of movements that will be perfected over a lifetime. Every time you mishandle dough, you squander days of work—not to mention nourishing food—so learning the stretching technique that harnesses the extensibility of the dough without overstressing the structure is key. There are lots of process shots in the recipes so you can learn the techniques more quickly. Remember, a busy *pizzaiolo* might make 400 pizzas in a night; it's tough to gain that type of experience in a home setting, so cheat a bit and watch YouTube videos of masters like Chris Bianco and mimic their subtle movements, which impose maximum impact with minimal intervention.

BAKING

In Italy, domed wood-fired ovens are used to bake Pizza Romana and Pizza Napoletana, while Pizza al Taglio is baked in electric deck ovens. Focaccia may be baked in either. Connecticut-Style Apizza is traditionally blasted in hot coal ovens (although many have been retrofitted with gas). In all cases, the pizzas are baked at very high temperatures that can't be replicated in a home oven. The doughs in this chapter have been developed so that they do work in home ovens while still remaining true to the texture and strength of their respective styles.

Home ovens reach 500°F to 550°F and you can best harness this heat with a baking stone. A baking stone will give your pizza a better crust, better volume, and incomparable lightness. If you do not have one, an inverted baking sheet or unglazed quarry tiles will work as substitutes. For the best results, preheat the stone or inverted baking sheet on the second-highest rack for at least 45 minutes before baking. Recipe cooking times depend upon your baking surface and will be shorter if you use a stone. Allow the stone to return to temperature between bakes, which may take 10 to 15 minutes.

An additional way to keep heat constant inside the oven is to fill the oven with cast-iron pots and pans and preheat them along with the stone.

PIZZA TOPPINGS

At the end of the chapter, I offer some of my favorite toppings. You can follow my recommendations for pairing toppings and pizza bases or mix and match as you like.

PIZZA AL TAGLIO

MAKES TWO 18 × 13-INCH PIZZAS

In Rome, *pizza al taglio*, or pizza by the slice, is sold by weight at bakeries and takeout places. The pizza is baked on sheet pans or slabs, then cut to order. It differs from an American slice in many ways, both in shape—*pizza al taglio* is square or rectangular—and in ingredients, but it's similar in that it's supposed to be quick, cheap fast food. But when I make it, I am not bogged down by the time and space constraints, not to mention the narrow profit margins, that cause most Roman *al taglio* joints to stick with mid- to low-quality ingredients. My approach is to ferment the dough for a long time so all the complex starch turns to simple starch, giving a crispier crust, more flavor, and more acidity. The result is so delicious that I want to eat it one tray—not one slice—at a time!

I prefer Iraq durum for its ability to capture carbon dioxide and the fact that it doesn't degrade during long fermentation the way another durum would (most durum wheats cannot be fermented for a long time, especially in the presence of a lot of water). When blended, Iraq durum and Red Fife team up to provide the strength needed for a wet dough—we're at 94% hydration. Also, Red Fife is really extensible, so it stretches nicely, and it has bold flavor. Prepare this dough 72 hours before baking.

VARIATION

Instead of durum and hard winter wheat, use 600 grams each of farro flour and Redeemer flour. The farro will give a ton of stretch, and its wheaty flavor profile will go really nicely with a range of toppings.

---

300 grams durum flour (I like Iraq), plus more for dusting

900 grams hard winter wheat flour (I like Red Fife)

888 grams tepid water

2½ grams active dry yeast

28 grams sea salt

Neutral oil (see page 62), for greasing

Desired toppings (see pages 200–205)

To "blind bake" pizza dough—that is, bake it without toppings—you want to be sure the dough is sufficiently pressed down and anchored to the pan as it won't have toppings to weigh it down for even cooking. To blind bake Pizza al Taglio, it is sufficient to make indentations all over the dough with your fingertips as the recipe instructs. To blind bake Bianco-Style Pizza for the Butter, Honey, and Lavender topping (page 205), push your fingertips hard into the dough all over except the edges. This will keep the dough from inflating irregularly as it bakes, while contributing to the thick rim.

In a large bowl, whisk together the durum and hard winter wheat flours.

Pour the water into the bowl of a stand mixer fitted with the dough hook, and then add the flour mixture. Mix on low speed until the flour is just incorporated, about 1 minute. Remove the dough hook and stir the bottom to ensure there is no unincorporated flour. If there is, continue mixing. Cover the bowl with plastic wrap and set the dough aside to hydrate at room temperature for 45 minutes.

Uncover the bowl, switch to the paddle attachment, and mix the dough on medium-low speed for 4 minutes. Add the yeast and salt, and mix on medium speed for

(recipe continues through page 181)

4 minutes, stopping occasionally to scrape down the sides of the bowl. Test the dough's strength with the "windowpane" test (see page 188). If you can see through the dough without breaking it, the dough is properly developed. Otherwise mix for 1 minute more, then test again. If after a total of 6 minutes of mixing the dough is not passing the test, set it aside for 15 minutes and try again.

With a bench scraper, loosen the dough from the sides of the bowl; then turn it out onto a work surface brushed sparingly with water.

PRE-SHAPE THE DOUGH: With two wet hands slightly tilted downward, lift the dough from the middle and let it hang. The dough will stretch as it hangs. Let the dough stretch down onto the work surface, then drop the middle part onto the resting hanging ends. Repeat the lifting,

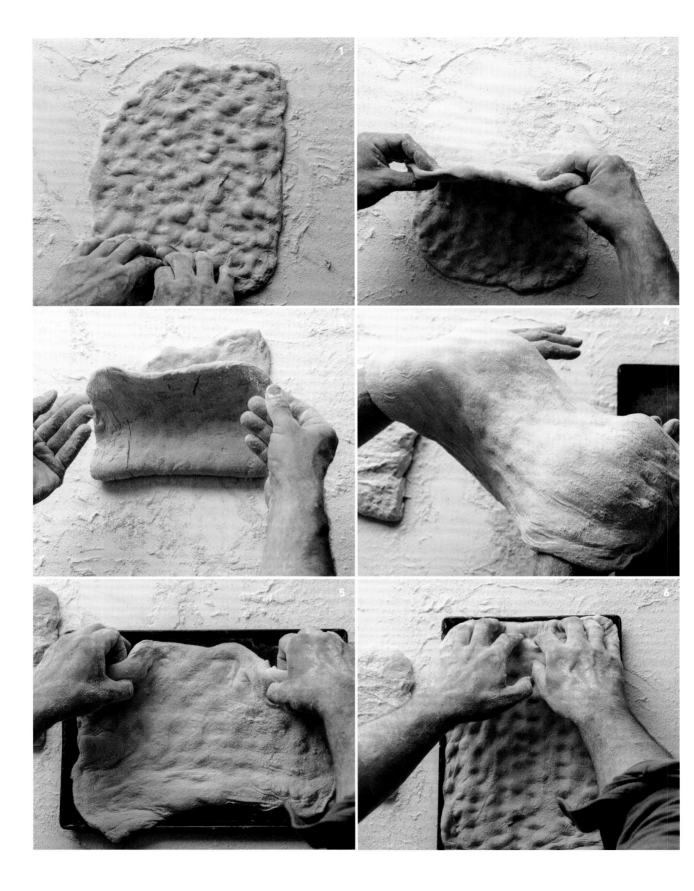

hanging, and dropping process once more. Drag the dough across the work surface toward you with both hands. Turn it 90 degrees and drag it again. Repeat the turning and dragging at least 4 and no more than 6 times, until you have a rough ball. Transfer the dough to a bowl, cover it with plastic wrap, and place it in the refrigerator to cold-ferment for about 24 hours.

The fermented dough will show signs such as bubbles on the surface and an airy structure. Uncover the bowl, and with two wet hands, repeat the lifting, hanging, and dropping process 2 more times.

Cut the dough in half with the bench scraper or a sharp knife. Transfer each dough ball to its own lightly greased medium bowl, cover each with plastic wrap, and return them to the refrigerator to ferment for another 48 hours. The fermented dough will have large bubbles on the surface. If it doesn't, continue to ferment at room temperature for 4 hours.

Preheat the oven to 500°F and set a baking stone or inverted baking sheet on the second-highest rack in the oven to preheat as well.

Grease two baking sheets and set them aside.

Carefully turn one dough ball out onto a lightly floured work surface, gently detaching it from the bowl with your fingers if necessary. Dust the top of the dough with flour. Then gently, starting at the top of the dough and working toward the bottom, press your fingertips into the dough (1). Flip the dough over (2) and, pressing more firmly, press the edges and then the center of the dough from top to bottom with your fingertips.

Dust the surface of the dough once more with flour. Fold the dough in half (3). Dust the exposed work surface with more flour. Return the folded part to the work surface, then repeat the folding and flour dusting with the other half. Transfer the dough to one of the prepared baking sheets (4). Fit the dough to the baking sheet by gently pushing it with spread fingertips, moving from the center outward (5). If it springs back, allow it to rest for a few minutes before trying again. Repeat with the remaining piece of dough. Set the dough aside to rest for 5 minutes.

With your fingertips, make indentations all over the dough to distribute the air pockets evenly (6), then add your choice of toppings.

Bake one pizza until the crust is golden with a few dark spots and the toppings are cooked, about 15 minutes. Set it aside to cool on a wire rack for a few minutes before slicing. Allow the oven temperature to return to 500°F before baking the second pizza.

Serve the pizza in slices or slivers.

PIZZA NAPOLETANA

MAKES FOUR 10-INCH PIZZAS

When I was a little kid growing up in Brooklyn, I thought New York–style pizza was a direct descendant of its ancestral Italian homeland. It wasn't until I began studying Italy's numerous styles—especially author and baking guru Peter Reinhart's account of bakeries in Italy—that I started to notice the defects of NYC pies, especially their flaccid crusts, sweet sauces, and oily toppings. At age twenty-six, I made my first trip to Naples. Equipped with a list of pizzerias given to me by acclaimed chef Michael White, I checked out a bunch of spots, and I was shocked. I couldn't believe the dough was so soft that it cooked in 60 seconds, that tomatoes could be so intense, and that the mozzarella was prized way more than the flour. My adoration of the New York pie waned as I started to understand what pizza can be when treated properly by a passionate *pizzaiolo* with a well-maintained oven and quality ingredients.

I think pizza should be accessible, so I have adapted this dough to work in a home oven—no need to invest in fancy equipment or a wood-burning pizza oven. I use Frederick soft spring wheat flour because it maintains that signature white hue, mild flavor, and soft crumb that is synonymous with Naples's most famous food. Prepare this dough 36 hours ahead of time.

630 grams water, warmed to 77°F

1,000 grams soft spring wheat flour (I like Frederick)

14 grams sea salt

2 grams active dry yeast

Neutral oil (see page 62), for greasing and brushing

Desired toppings (see pages 200–205)

Pour the water into the bowl of a stand mixer fitted with the dough hook, and then add the flour. Mix on low speed until the flour is incorporated, about 1 minute. Scrape down the sides of the bowl. Add just the salt and the yeast and mix on medium speed for 6 minutes, stopping occasionally to scrape down the sides and bottom of the mixing bowl. Continue on high speed for 2 minutes. Cover the bowl with plastic wrap and set it aside at room temperature for 3 hours.

With a bench scraper, loosen the dough from the sides of the bowl, then turn it out onto a work surface brushed sparingly with water. With the bench scraper or a sharp knife, divide the dough into 4 pieces, each weighing about 330 grams.

Place the palm of your hand on top of one piece of dough, resting your thumb and pinkie against the sides and your other fingertips on the counter. Gently move the ball in circles to form a sphere, taking care to prevent any tears. Repeat this process with the remaining dough pieces.

Place the shaped dough balls on a greased baking sheet. Brush the dough lightly with neutral oil and cover the whole sheet with plastic wrap. Transfer it to the refrigerator and allow the dough to cold-ferment for 36 hours. The fermented dough will show signs of active fermentation such as bubbles on its surface and an airy structure. If not, discard the dough and begin again.

Three hours before baking, remove the dough from the refrigerator and allow it to come to room temperature, still covered. The dough will rise slightly as it warms.

(recipe continues through page 185)

Preheat the oven to 500°F and set a baking stone or inverted baking sheet on the second-highest rack in the oven to preheat as well.

Place one dough ball on a well-floured surface, then sprinkle more flour on top. Start working the dough into a small disk by pushing your fingertips flat into the dough (1), leaving the edge untouched and the center portion just slightly higher. Continue until you have a round disk about 6 inches in diameter (2). Flip the disk over and move it to a portion of the work surface that is just lightly floured.

Place both hands on top, palms down, side by side. Use one hand to gently pull the dough away from the center, working slowly and carefully to prevent tearing (3). Add a light dusting of flour to the work surface if the dough begins to stick. Give the dough a one-eighth turn and repeat, repositioning your hands. Continue until the disk is about 10 inches in diameter with a thick rim around the edge. Finally, push your fingertips hard into the dough all over except for the rim. This will keep the dough from inflating irregularly as it bakes, while contributing to the signature thick crust of the Neapolitan pizza style.

Transfer the shaped dough to a pizza peel or a parchment-lined inverted baking sheet. Add your choice of toppings and transfer the pizza to the preheated baking stone. Bake until the crust is slightly charred around the edges and the toppings are cooked, 6 to 10 minutes. Slice and serve immediately.

Repeat with the remaining dough balls, allowing the oven to return to 500°F before baking each pizza.

PIZZA ROMANA

MAKES FOUR 12- TO 15-INCH PIZZAS

In addition to being Italy's best bread (just the facts, folks), pizza is also the country's most famous export. Not every city has its own style, but many do and places like Naples have been defined by their native flatbread. I dig Roman style. Pizza makers in the Italian capital barely ferment their dough and I love the chewy, crispy, thin-crusted results. While Roman pizzerias rarely ferment their dough for more than 6 hours, I have extended the proofing time to accommodate Edison, a heady hard winter wheat, which cold-ferments for 24 to 48 hours. Just as with the Pizza al Taglio (page 175), we don't have the limitations of Rome's narrow-profit-margin pizzerias, which have to move product fast, so we can develop flavor through fermentation. The small amount of Magog adds a nice earthy undertone.

1 scant gram active dry yeast

280 grams cold water

450 grams hard winter wheat flour (I like Edison), plus more for dusting

50 grams Magog wheat flour

12 grams sea salt

12 grams extra-virgin olive oil

Neutral oil (see page 62), for greasing and brushing

Desired toppings (see pages 200–205)

In a small bowl, sprinkle the yeast over the cold water. Set the bowl aside for a few minutes until the yeast has dissolved.

In a medium bowl, whisk together the hard winter wheat and Magog flours.

Pour the yeast mixture into the bowl of a stand mixer fitted with the dough hook, and then add the flour mixture. Mix on low speed until the dough comes together, about 3 minutes, stopping occasionally to scrape down the sides of the bowl. Set the dough aside for 5 minutes to hydrate. Then add the salt and mix on medium speed for 4 minutes, or until the dough is smooth and has developed good elasticity. With the mixer running on medium speed, slowly add the olive oil and mix until incorporated.

Cover the bowl with plastic wrap and allow the dough to rest for about 30 minutes at room temperature.

With a bench scraper, loosen the dough from the sides of the bowl and turn it out onto a lightly floured work surface. With the bench scraper or a sharp knife, cut it into 4 equal pieces.

Working with one piece of dough at a time, take four edges and pull and fold them into the center. Do not flatten. The dough will tighten up and take on a round shape. Flip the dough seam-side down on the work surface. Place the palm of your hand on top of the ball, resting your thumb and pinkie against the sides and your other fingertips on the counter. Gently move the ball to form a sphere, taking care to prevent any tears. Repeat this process with the remaining dough pieces.

Place the shaped dough balls on a greased baking sheet. Brush them lightly with neutral oil and cover the whole baking sheet with plastic wrap. Transfer it to the refrigerator and allow the dough to cold-ferment for at least 24 and up to 48 hours. The fermented dough will show signs of active fermentation such as bubbles on its surface and an airy structure. If not, discard the dough and begin again.

Three hours before baking, remove the dough from the refrigerator and allow it to come to room temperature, still covered. The dough will rise slightly as it warms.

Preheat the oven to 500°F and set a baking stone or inverted baking sheet on the second-highest rack in the oven to preheat as well.

Place one dough ball on a well-floured surface, then sprinkle more flour on top. Start working the dough into a small disk by pushing your fingertips near the center of the dough and radiating outward toward the edges, leaving the center just slightly higher. Continue until you have a round disk about 6 inches in diameter and ¼ inch thick. Flip the disk over and move it to a portion of the work surface that is just lightly floured.

Place both hands on top, palms down, side by side. Use one hand to gently pull the dough away from the center, working slowly and carefully to prevent tearing. Add a light dusting of flour to the work surface if the dough begins to stick. Give the dough a one-quarter turn and repeat, repositioning your hands. Continue until the disk is 12 to 15 inches in diameter and as thin as possible without tearing.

Transfer the shaped dough to a pizza peel or a parchment-lined inverted baking sheet. Add your choice of toppings and transfer the pizza to the preheated baking stone. Bake until the crust is crisp and the toppings are cooked, 8 to 9 minutes. Slice and serve immediately.

Repeat with the remaining dough, allowing the oven to return to 500°F before baking each pizza.

CONNECTICUT-STYLE APIZZA
MAKES TWO 18-INCH APIZZAS

As the name suggests, Connecticut-style pizza was pioneered in the Constitution State. It was put on the map by rival New Haven pizzerias Pepe's and Sally's. The dough for Connecticut pies, called "apizza" locally, is similar to that of pizza Napoletana, but the resulting pies are much bigger, lack a raised crust, and are cooked in coal-fired ovens, which get crazy hot. The heat comes from the bottom—hot steel powered by coal—which allows you to add more water and stretch a larger round of dough that can still bake evenly and get crispy. In fact, it gets way crispier than a pizza Napoletana, and it spends more time in the oven—so it gives you time to add toppings that take longer to cook, like clams, the quintessential apizza condiment.

My top spot in New Haven is Frank Pepe's Pizzeria, located in the historic Wooster Square district, though it has expanded to a multi-location empire. In addition to trying this and Sally's Apizza, I also recommend BAR, a brew pub and pizzeria on Crown Street in downtown New Haven, and Modern Apizza. To re-create apizza at home, I like using Red Fife flour because at 10.5% protein, it has just enough strength to give this pizza what it needs to hold its shape and because it continues to "lift" while cooking, which is ideal for cooking heavier toppings. Plus it has a great wheat flavor. Prepare this dough 72 hours before baking.

375 grams cold water

500 grams hard winter wheat flour (I like Red Fife), plus more for dusting

10 grams extra-virgin olive oil

5 grams fresh compact yeast

12 grams sea salt

Neutral oil (see page 62), for greasing and brushing

Desired toppings (see pages 200–205)

THE WINDOWPANE TEST
To test a dough's strength, cut off a little piece, roll the dough into a ball with floured hands, and then gently stretch it (without tearing!) into a square "windowpane" shape. This test was invented by an anonymous genius to let you know whether the dough has developed properly. If you can see through the stretched dough without breaking it, the dough is ready to use.

Pour the water into the bowl of a stand mixer fitted with the dough hook, and then add the flour. Mix on low speed for 8 minutes, stopping occasionally to scrape down the sides of the bowl. Add the olive oil and the yeast, and mix on medium speed for 6 minutes, adding the salt a little at a time. Mix on high speed for 2 minutes. Test for strength with the "windowpane" test (see note). Cover the bowl with plastic wrap and transfer the dough to the refrigerator to cold-ferment for 72 hours. After 24 hours have passed, remove the dough from the refrigerator and unwrap. With one wet hand, lightly grasp one edge of the dough. Give the bowl a one-eighth turn and repeat for a full turn. Cover the bowl with plastic wrap and return to the refrigerator for the remaining time. The fermented dough will show

signs of active fermentation such as bubbles on its surface and an airy structure. If not, discard the dough and begin again.

With a bench scraper, loosen the dough from the sides of the bowl and turn it out onto a lightly floured work surface. Cut the dough in half with the bench scraper or a sharp knife. Place the palm of your hand on top of one piece of dough, resting your thumb and pinkie against the sides and your other fingertips on the counter. Gently move the dough in circles to form a sphere, taking care to prevent any tears. Repeat this process with the remaining dough. Place the dough balls on a greased baking sheet. Brush the dough lightly with neutral oil and cover the whole baking sheet with plastic wrap. Set it aside to reach room temperature and to rest for 1 hour.

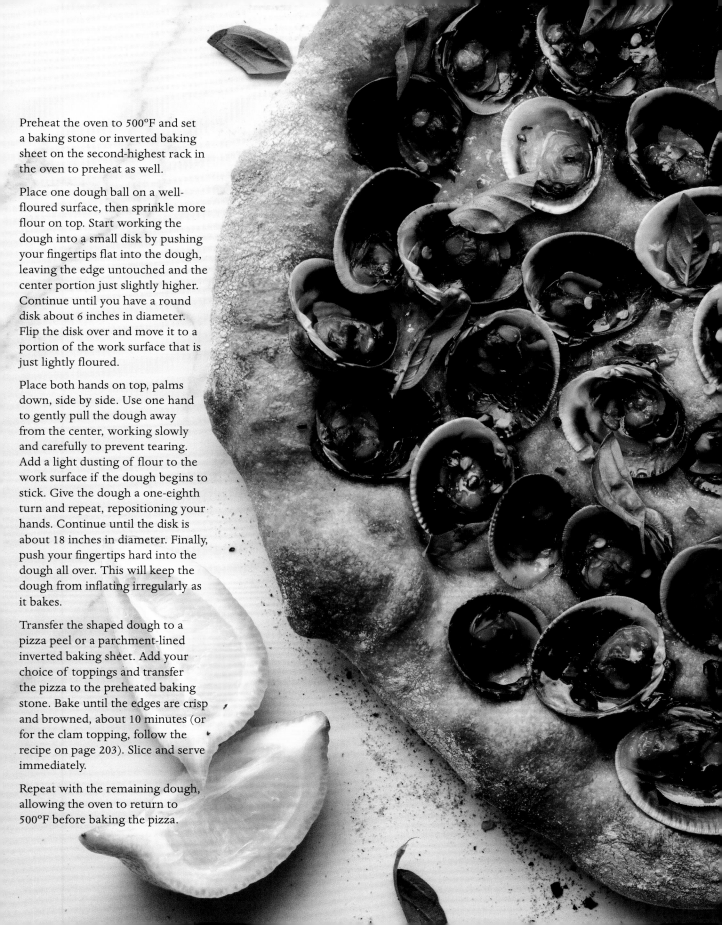

Preheat the oven to 500°F and set a baking stone or inverted baking sheet on the second-highest rack in the oven to preheat as well.

Place one dough ball on a well-floured surface, then sprinkle more flour on top. Start working the dough into a small disk by pushing your fingertips flat into the dough, leaving the edge untouched and the center portion just slightly higher. Continue until you have a round disk about 6 inches in diameter. Flip the disk over and move it to a portion of the work surface that is just lightly floured.

Place both hands on top, palms down, side by side. Use one hand to gently pull the dough away from the center, working slowly and carefully to prevent tearing. Add a light dusting of flour to the work surface if the dough begins to stick. Give the dough a one-eighth turn and repeat, repositioning your hands. Continue until the disk is about 18 inches in diameter. Finally, push your fingertips hard into the dough all over. This will keep the dough from inflating irregularly as it bakes.

Transfer the shaped dough to a pizza peel or a parchment-lined inverted baking sheet. Add your choice of toppings and transfer the pizza to the preheated baking stone. Bake until the edges are crisp and browned, about 10 minutes (or for the clam topping, follow the recipe on page 203). Slice and serve immediately.

Repeat with the remaining dough, allowing the oven to return to 500°F before baking the pizza.

DETROIT-STYLE PIZZA

MAKES TWO 18 × 13-INCH PIZZAS

Detroit-style pizza was born in the 1940s when Anna Passalacqua, owner of the Cloverleaf bar, baked *sfincione*, a subtly sweet Sicilian flatbread, in a pan intended for car parts—the Motor City's automotive spirit finding a way even into its food. Topped with tomato sauce, mozzarella, and pepperoni, the deep-dish pie has recently migrated from its city of origin to places like Descendant in Toronto and Emmy Squared in Brooklyn. This twist on the original uses a modified focaccia base; the Kansas Turkey wheat gives the dough strength, while the low-gluten rye imparts tenderness and lends a sweetness that reflects the flavor of the original *sfincione*.

960 grams hard red winter wheat flour (I like Kansas Turkey)

400 grams rye flour

1,140 grams tepid water

44 grams sea salt

5 grams active dry yeast

Neutral oil (see page 62), for brushing

Extra-virgin olive oil, for greasing and brushing

Desired toppings (see pages 200–205)

In a large bowl, whisk together the hard red winter wheat and rye flours.

Pour the water into the bowl of a stand mixer fitted with the paddle attachment, and then add the flour mixture. Mix on low speed for 4 minutes, until the dough takes on the consistency of cheese curds. Stop to scrape down the sides of the bowl. Add the salt and the yeast, and mix on medium-high speed for 2 minutes. Cover the bowl with plastic wrap and set it aside at room temperature until the dough has doubled in size, about 2 hours.

Uncover the bowl. With a bench scraper, loosen the dough from the sides of the bowl and turn it out onto a surface brushed sparingly with neutral oil.

With your fingertips, press the dough all over, with enough pressure to deflate but not tear it. Work the dough gently into a roughly rectangular shape. Cut the dough in half with the bench scraper or a sharp knife.

Transfer each piece of dough to its own baking sheet greased generously with olive oil. Working from the center to the edges, gently stretch the dough to match the size of the sheets. Liberally brush the surface of each dough with olive oil and use the tips of your fingers to spread it out. Set the dough aside, uncovered, at room temperature for 90 minutes. The dough should double in size. If it does not, allow it to sit at room temperature for 30 minutes more.

Meanwhile, preheat the oven to 500°F and set a baking stone or inverted baking sheet on the second-highest rack in the oven to preheat as well.

Add your choice of toppings. Transfer the baking sheets to the oven and bake for 20 to 25 minutes. Reduce the heat to 300°F and bake for 15 minutes more, until the crust is golden. Slice into squares on the sheets and serve immediately.

PROVIDENCE-STYLE PIZZA

MAKES FOUR 12- TO 15-INCH PIZZAS

This recipe is an homage to the pizzeria Al Forno in Providence, Rhode Island, where Johanne Killeen and George Germon began grilling pizza rather than baking it over three decades ago. While New Haven and New York styles are widely touted, Providence flies under the radar and Killeen and Germon never got the nationwide recognition they deserved for their innovative cooking technique. What's really fun about grilling pizza is that it lets you cook the dough at a temperature that far exceeds the heat of a home oven. Here, with just your run-of-the-mill backyard grill, you get intense heat, which "lifts" the dough as it cooks, giving it a lighter interior structure.

Similar to the classic dough for Roman-style pizza, Al Forno's dough is fermented for a very short time. The pizza base is thin, crispy, and chewy, and barely has a crust. In order to accommodate freshly milled flour, this modified Al Forno dough ferments for 36 hours. The soft spring wheat flour gives it a delicate structure and pleasant chewiness, which will have you looking for tickets to Providence after one bite.

1 gram active dry yeast

280 grams cold water

500 grams soft spring wheat flour (I like Sonora), plus more for dusting

12 grams sea salt

12 grams extra-virgin olive oil, plus more for greasing and brushing

Neutral oil (see page 62), for greasing and brushing

Desired toppings (see pages 200–205)

In a small bowl, sprinkle the yeast over the cold water. Set the bowl aside for a few minutes until the yeast has dissolved.

Pour the yeast mixture into the bowl of a stand mixer fitted with the dough hook, and then add the flour. Mix on low speed until the dough comes together, about 3 minutes, stopping occasionally to scrape down the sides of the bowl. Set the dough aside for 5 minutes to hydrate. Then add the salt and mix on medium speed for 4 minutes, or until the dough is smooth and has developed good elasticity. With the mixer running on medium speed, slowly add the olive oil and mix until incorporated.

Cover the bowl with plastic wrap and allow the dough to rest for about 30 minutes at room temperature.

With a bench scraper, loosen the dough from the sides of the bowl and turn it out onto a lightly floured surface. With the bench scraper

or a sharp knife, cut it into 4 equal pieces.

Working with one piece of dough at a time, take four edges and pull and fold them into the center. Do not flatten. The dough will tighten up and take on a round shape. Flip the dough seam-side down on the work surface. Place the palm of your hand on top of the ball, resting your thumb and pinkie against the sides and your other fingertips on the counter. Gently move the ball to form a sphere, taking care to prevent any tears. Repeat this process with the remaining dough.

Place the shaped dough balls on a greased baking sheet. Brush them lightly with neutral oil and cover the whole baking sheet with plastic wrap. Transfer it to the refrigerator and allow the dough to cold-ferment for at least 36 hours. The fermented dough will show signs of active fermentation such as bubbles on its surface and an airy structure. If not, discard the dough and begin again.

(recipe continues through page 193)

Three hours before baking, remove the dough from the refrigerator and allow it to come to room temperature, still covered. The dough will rise slightly as it warms.

Twenty minutes before the dough is ready, fire up your grill to its highest temperature.

Place one dough ball on a well-floured surface, then sprinkle more flour on top. Start working the dough into a small disk by pushing your fingertips near the center of the dough and radiating outward toward the edges, leaving the center just slightly higher. Continue until you have a round disk about 6 inches in diameter and ¼ inch thick. Flip the disk over and move it to a portion of the work surface that is just lightly floured. With a rolling pin, roll from the center away from you to 12 o'clock. Give the disk a one-eighth turn and repeat until you have rotated the disk a complete turn. The dough will be 12 to 15 inches in diameter.

Transfer the shaped dough to a pizza peel or a parchment-lined inverted baking sheet and slide it onto the grill grate. Cook over medium heat, resisting the temptation to move or check the dough; it will release from the grate when it is ready. Grill for 2 to 3 minutes, flip the dough, and add your choice of toppings. Close the lid and grill for 3 minutes, or until the dough is cooked through, the bottom has grill marks, and the dough releases itself from the grill. Slice and serve immediately.

Repeat with the remaining dough.

FOCACCIA

MAKES ONE 18 × 13-INCH FOCACCIA

Focaccia is one of those Italian words that means something different depending on where you use it—literally. In Liguria, it's an oil-rich, dry-crumbed, dimpled flatbread, while in the extreme southern region of Puglia, it's more like a thick, airy, spongy bread. This version, made with *biga*, a classic Italian pre-ferment, is inspired by the flatbreads of Bari and central Puglia. Sticking to the Pugliese tradition of blending durum with other flours to compensate for durum's low starch quality, this recipe employs the relatively neutral-flavored Redeemer wheat for its strength, letting the Iraq durum's intense flavor come through while contributing to the dough's structure. The result is thick and rich and meant to be enjoyed with complete abandon. Pair it with a generous stack of paper napkins.

340 grams hard red wheat flour (I like Redeemer)

340 grams durum wheat flour (I like Iraq)

570 grams tepid water

Focaccia Biga (recipe follows)

3 grams active dry yeast

22 grams sea salt

Neutral oil (see page 62), for brushing

Extra-virgin olive oil, for greasing and brushing

Flaky sea salt (I like Maldon)

In a large bowl, whisk together the hard red wheat and durum flours. Pour the water into the bowl of a stand mixer fitted with the paddle attachment, and then add the flour mixture and the *biga*. Mix on medium speed for 4 minutes, until the dough takes on the consistency of cheese curds. Stop occasionally to scrape down the sides of the bowl. Replace the paddle with the dough hook. Add the yeast, and mix on medium-high speed for 2 minutes while slowly adding the salt. Cover the bowl with plastic wrap and set it aside at room temperature until the dough has doubled in size, about 2 hours.

Uncover the bowl. With a bench scraper, loosen the dough from the sides of the bowl and turn it out onto a surface brushed sparingly with neutral oil.

With your fingertips, press the dough all over, with enough pressure to deflate but not tear it. Work the dough gently into a roughly rectangular shape.

Transfer the dough to a baking sheet greased generously with olive oil. Working from the center to the edges, gently stretch the dough to match the size of the sheet. Liberally brush the surface of the dough with olive oil and use the tips of your fingers to spread it out. Set the dough aside, uncovered, at room temperature, until it has fermented and risen by about 40%, 90 minutes or more.

Preheat the oven to 500°F and set a baking stone or inverted baking sheet on the second-highest rack in the oven to preheat as well.

Sprinkle the flaky sea salt to taste over the dough. Place the baking sheet with the dough on the preheated baking stone or baking sheet, and bake until it is a light golden brown, about 10 minutes. Reduce the heat to 350°F and bake until the crust is golden all over and springs back when pressed, about 20 minutes. Brush it with additional olive oil and serve warm, in slices or slivers.

(recipe continues through page 197)

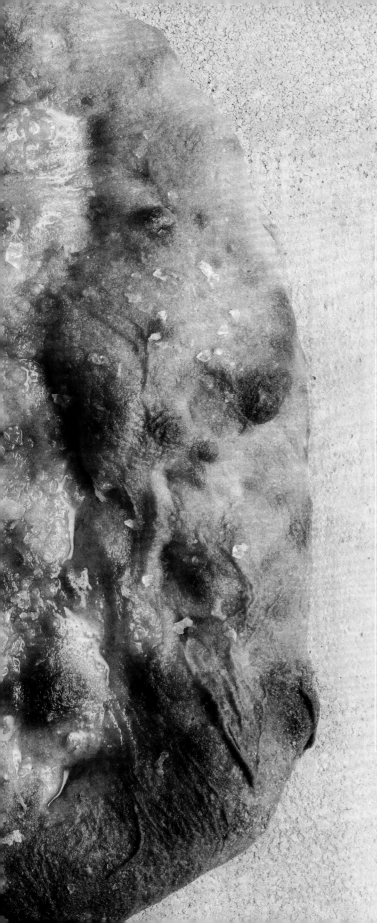

FOCACCIA BIGA

385 grams cool water

550 grams Redeemer wheat flour

3 grams active dry yeast

Neutral oil (see page 62), for greasing

Pour the water into the bowl of a stand mixer fitted with the dough hook and add the flour, then the yeast. Mix on medium speed for 4 minutes, stopping occasionally to scrape down the sides of the bowl. Continue on high speed for 2 minutes. The dough should be fairly dry.

Transfer the *biga* to a lightly oiled large bowl, cover it with plastic wrap, and set it aside at room temperature to ferment for 3 hours.

Check for signs of fermentation, such as bubbles on the surface and around the edges of the mixture. Refrigerate the *biga*, covered, overnight. It will keep for up to 2 days in a sealed container in the refrigerator.

BIANCO-STYLE PIZZA

MAKES FOUR 12-INCH PIZZAS

This pizza was inspired by Chris Bianco, living pizza Hall of Famer and owner of Pizzeria Bianco, Pane Bianco, and Tratto in Phoenix. Years ago, when I was visiting the Bread Lab at Washington State University with Marc Vetri, I had one of the best days of my life. Dough royalty Chad Robertson of Tartine and Chris Bianco were both there, too. All my baking heroes in one place—no big deal. We started playing around with different flours, and the Lab's resident baker and flour genius Jonathan Bethany-McDowell asked Chris to give him a crash course in pizza making. Chris was tight on time, but in accordance with his intensely generous spirit, he obliged and asked Jonathan if he had any really ripe levain to speed up the fermentation process. Jonathan dug some up and Chris made a dough with 30% levain by weight—a huge proportion compared with the average 14%. It fermented fully in just 2 hours, a clever solution to making a flavorful pizza on a tight schedule. Thanks to Chris's creativity and expert handling, it was one of the best pizzas I have ever tasted. Chris used a ton of salt to tame the levain in this high-hydration dough. Normally I shoot for 2% salt in my pizza doughs, but I bump it up to 3.2% here. The choice of Redeemer wheat, which has a neutral to medium flavor, really lets the levain take over the pizza's flavor profile; the levain contributes other characteristics, too, like a shinier dough than usual.

450 grams tepid water

500 grams hard winter wheat flour (I like Redeemer), plus more for dusting

150 grams Levain (page 90)

16 grams sea salt

Desired toppings (see pages 200–205)

Combine the water, flour, levain, and salt in a large bowl, and using your hands, mix just until the dough comes together. Set aside to rest, covered with plastic wrap, to hydrate for 5 minutes. Uncover the bowl. With one wet hand, lightly grasp one edge of the dough. Pull this flap of dough upward and outward, then attach it to the top of the dough. Give the bowl a one-eighth turn and repeat this process for 5 minutes. Cover the bowl with plastic wrap and set it aside to rest for 15 minutes. Uncover the bowl and repeat the pulling, lifting, and turning for another 2 minutes. Repeat this process every 15 minutes for 1 hour, a total of 4 times.

With a bench scraper, loosen the dough from the sides of the bowl, and turn it out onto a well-floured surface. With the bench scraper or a sharp knife, cut the dough in

quarters. Working with one piece of dough, fold the dough in half. Gripping the far end, pull the dough toward you. Turn it 90 degrees, then drag it toward you again. Repeat the drag-and-pull procedure about 4 times, until the dough forms a nice tight ball. Repeat with the remaining pieces of dough. Set the dough balls aside, uncovered, to rest until the dough no longer springs back when pressed, 15 to 30 minutes.

Preheat the oven to 500°F and set a baking stone or inverted baking sheet on the second-highest rack in the oven to preheat as well.

Place one dough ball on a well-floured surface, then sprinkle more flour on top. Start working the dough into a small disk by pushing your fingertips flat into the dough, leaving the edge untouched and the center portion just slightly higher. Continue until you have a round disk about 6 inches in diameter and about ¾ inch thick. Flip the disk over and move it to a portion of the work surface that is just lightly floured.

Place both hands on top, palms down, side by side. Use one hand to gently pull the dough away from the center, working slowly and carefully to prevent tearing. Add a light dusting of flour to the work surface if the dough begins to stick. Give the dough a one-eighth turn and repeat, repositioning your hands. Continue until the disk is about 12 inches in diameter with a thick crust around the edge. Finally, push your fingertips hard into the dough all over except the crust. This will keep the dough from inflating irregularly as it bakes, while contributing to the thick rim.

Transfer the shaped dough to a pizza peel or a parchment-lined inverted baking sheet. Add your choice of toppings and transfer the pizza to the preheated baking stone. Bake until the crust is slightly charred around the edges and the toppings are cooked, 6 to 8 minutes. Slice and serve immediately.

Repeat with the remaining dough, allowing the oven to return to 500°F before baking the pizza.

PIZZA TOPPINGS

BROCCOLI RABE AND PECORINO TOSCANO

Best for one 18 × 13-inch
Pizza al Taglio (page 175).

60 grams (about 2 ounces) broccoli rabe, fibrous stalks discarded

115 grams (about 4 ounces) Pecorino Toscano, shaved

Red pepper flakes

Sea salt

Extra-virgin olive oil

Distribute the whole broccoli rabe leaves evenly over the dough, nearly to the edge, followed by the Pecorino. Season with red pepper flakes and salt to taste. Drizzle generously with olive oil. Bake the pizza as described in the recipe.

ROBIOLA, MORTADELLA, AND ARUGULA

Best for one 18 × 13-inch
Pizza al Taglio (page 175).

450 grams (16 ounces) Robiola cheese

200 grams (7 ounces) mortadella, thinly sliced

40 grams (2½ ounces) arugula

Extra-virgin olive oil

Spread the Robiola over the warm crust of a blind-baked (see page 175) Pizza al Taglio. Distribute the slices of mortadella evenly. Top with the arugula, and drizzle generously with olive oil. Slice and serve immediately.

HERBS AND OIL

Best for one 18 × 13-inch
Pizza al Taglio (page 175).

40 grams (about 1½ ounces) flat-leaf Italian parsley, leaves only

20 grams (about ¾ ounce) finely chopped fresh sage

20 grams (about ¾ ounce) finely chopped fresh rosemary

Leaves from 12 sprigs fresh thyme

100 grams (about ½ cup) extra-virgin olive oil

Sea salt

Freshly ground black pepper

In a medium bowl, combine the parsley, sage, rosemary, thyme, and olive oil and stir until incorporated. Distribute the mixture evenly over the dough. Season with salt and pepper to taste. Bake the pizza as described in the recipe.

TOMATO AND STRACCIATELLA

Best for one 10-inch
Pizza Napoletana (page 182).

115 grams (½ cup) whole peeled
Piennolo or Corbara tomatoes,
crushed by hand

150 grams (about 5 ounces)
stracciatella di burrata cheese

Rock salt

Generous pinch of chopped fresh
oregano

14 grams (about 1 tablespoon) extra-
virgin olive oil

Distribute the tomatoes over the pizza
dough, leaving a ½-inch border. Then
distribute the stracciatella evenly over
the tomatoes. Season with salt to taste.
Bake the pizza as described in the
recipe.

After baking, garnish with the oregano
and drizzle with the olive oil.

MUSHROOMS

Best for one 10-inch
Pizza Napoletana (page 182).

115 grams (about ½ cup) tomato sauce

100 grams (about 4 ounces)
mushrooms (I like cremini), thinly
sliced

70 grams (2½ ounces) mozzarella,
torn or cut into ½-inch pieces

Spoon the tomato sauce over the
pizza dough, leaving a ½-inch border,
then distribute the mushrooms and
mozzarella evenly. Bake the pizza as
described in the recipe.

SAUSAGE AND BROCCOLINI

Best for one 10-inch
Pizza Napoletana (page 182).

Sea salt

100 grams (4 ounces) broccolini

150 grams (5 ounces) spicy sausage,
casings removed, chopped

70 grams (2½ ounces) mozzarella,
torn or cut into ½-inch pieces

Bring a large pot of water to a boil over
high heat. Salt the water. When the salt
has dissolved, add the broccolini. Boil
until tender and cooked through, about
4 minutes. Drain and set aside to cool.
When the broccolini is cool enough to
handle, squeeze out any excess water
and coarsely chop it.

Distribute the sausage, broccolini,
and mozzarella over the pizza dough,
leaving a ½-inch border. Bake the pizza
as described in the recipe.

FOUR CHEESES

Best for one 18-inch Connecticut-
Style Apizza (page 188).

225 grams (8 ounces) mozzarella, torn
or cut into ½-inch pieces

100 grams (3½ ounces) Gorgonzola,
crumbled

100 grams (3½ ounces) grated
Pecorino Romano

100 grams (3½ ounces) fontina,
shaved

Distribute the mozzarella, Gorgonzola,
Pecorino, and fontina over the pizza
dough. Bake the pizza as described in
the recipe.

CLAMS

Best for one 18-inch Connecticut-
Style Apizza (page 188).

70 grams (¼ cup plus 1 tablespoon)
extra-virgin olive oil

3 garlic cloves

1,125 grams (about 2½ pounds) fresh
clams (I like cherrystones or cockles)

350 grams (1½ cups) dry white wine

1 bunch parsley, leaves only, coarsely
chopped

Red pepper flakes

1 lemon, cut into wedges

Heat the ¼ cup olive oil in a large
skillet over low heat. When the oil
begins to shimmer, add the garlic. Cook
the garlic just until it starts to take
on color, about 6 minutes, and then
discard the cloves.

Add the clams and the white wine to
the oil in the skillet. Simmer until the
clams just open, about 5 minutes.
Remove the clams and set aside on
a tray. Meanwhile, raise the heat to
high and reduce the liquid in the pan
to ½ cup. Remove from the heat and
set aside.

Distribute the clams in their shells
over the pizza dough. Bake the pizza as
described in the recipe for 6 minutes.
Then remove the pizza from the oven
and distribute the reduced liquid and
parsley on top. Return the pizza to the
oven to finish cooking, about 6 minutes.
Serve immediately, seasoned with red
pepper flakes and with the remaining
olive oil drizzled on top and the lemon
wedges alongside.

GRICIA

Best for one 18-inch Connecticut-Style Apizza (page 188).

14 grams (1 tablespoon) extra-virgin olive oil

40 grams (1½ ounces) pancetta, cut into ⅛-inch-thick tiles

70 grams (2½ ounces) mozzarella, torn or cut into ½-inch pieces

Freshly ground black pepper

Heat the olive oil in a small pan over medium heat. When the oil begins to shimmer, add the pancetta. Cook, stirring frequently, until lightly browned, about 2 minutes. Transfer the pancetta to paper towels to drain for a few minutes.

Distribute the pancetta, mozzarella, and pepper evenly over the pizza dough. Bake the pizza as described in the recipe and serve immediately.

PISTACHIO PESTO AND FONTINA

Best for one 12- to 15-inch Pizza Romana (page 186).

125 grams (1 cup) unsalted pistachios, hulled

215 grams (1 cup) grapeseed oil

Sea salt

100 grams (3½ ounces) fontina, shaved

Healthy pinch of fresh thyme leaves

5 grams (1 teaspoon) red wine vinegar

Combine the pistachios, the oil, and salt to taste in the bowl of a food processor and blend until the mixture has the consistency of chunky peanut butter.

Distribute the pesto over the pizza dough, spreading it to the edge of the crust. Bake the pizza as described in the recipe.

After baking, lay the fontina over the pesto. Garnish with the thyme, drizzle with the vinegar, and serve immediately.

CORN WITH SCALLIONS

Best for one 12- to 15-inch Providence-Style Pizza (page 191).

30 grams (2 tablespoons) extra-virgin olive oil

2 grams (1 teaspoon) red pepper flakes

1 whole scallion, thinly sliced

1 ear of corn, kernels sliced off and reserved

Sea salt

45 grams (1½ ounces) ricotta salata, shaved

3 sprigs fresh parsley, leaves only

¼ lime

Heat the olive oil in a medium skillet over medium heat. When the oil begins to shimmer, add the red pepper flakes. Cook until fragrant, about 30 seconds, then add the scallion and the corn kernels. Season with salt and cook, stirring, until softened, about 2 minutes.

Spoon the corn mixture over the partially grilled dough almost to the edge. Continue with the pizza recipe. Garnish the grilled pizza with the ricotta salata and parsley, and squeeze the lime all over.

PEPPERONI

Best for one 18 × 13-inch
Detroit-Style Pizza (page 190).

**400 grams (2 cups) whole canned
tomatoes, crushed by hand**

**8 grams (2 teaspoons) turbinado
sugar, such as Sugar in the Raw**

**115 grams (4 ounces) thinly sliced
pepperoni**

**170 grams (6 ounces) Wisconsin brick
cheese or low-moisture mozzarella,
shredded**

In a medium bowl, combine the
tomatoes and sugar and mix well.
With a ladle or your hands, spread
the tomato mixture over the stretched
pizza dough in an even layer, nearly
to the edge of the dough. Distribute
the pepperoni slices over the tomato
sauce, and then sprinkle the cheese
over the pepperoni. Continue with the
pizza recipe.

TOMATO AND OLIVE

Best for one 18 × 13-inch
Detroit-Style Pizza (page 190).

**1½ grams (1½ teaspoons) dried
oregano**

**250 grams (1¾ cups) ripe cherry
tomatoes, halved**

¼ cup pitted black olives

Sprinkle the oregano onto the
stretched pizza dough. Gently press in
the cherry tomatoes, cut-side down,
and the olives, distributing them
evenly. Continue with the pizza recipe.

MEAT LOVERS

Best for one 18 × 13-inch
Detroit-Style Pizza (page 190).

230 grams (1 cup) tomato sauce

150 grams (5 ounces) ground beef

**150 grams (5 ounces) bacon, cut into
¼-inch-thick tiles**

**150 grams (5 ounces) spicy sausage,
casings removed, chopped**

¼ white onion, diced

½ green bell pepper, diced

**225 grams (8 ounces) mozzarella, torn
or cut into ½-inch pieces**

Spoon the tomato sauce over the
stretched pizza dough, and then evenly
distribute the ground beef, bacon,
sausage, onion, bell pepper, and
mozzarella. Continue with the pizza
recipe.

BUTTER, HONEY, AND LAVENDER

Best for one 12-inch
Bianco-Style Pizza (page 198).

**100 grams (3½ ounces) unsalted
butter**

15 grams (about 2 tablespoons) honey

**2 grams (1 tablespoon) dried culinary
lavender**

Spread the butter all over the blind-
baked pizza (see page 175). Drizzle
with the honey. Distribute the lavender
evenly, and serve.

GARLIC AND HERB

Best for one 12-inch
Bianco-Style Pizza (page 198).

**Cloves from 1 head of garlic, sliced
super-thin**

**15 grams (1 tablespoon) extra-virgin
olive oil**

3 sprigs fresh thyme

**1 sprig fresh rosemary, leaves only,
finely chopped**

2 tablespoons finely chopped chives

Sea salt

Distribute the garlic slices and the
olive oil over the pizza dough to the
edge of the raised crust. Bake as
described in the pizza recipe for
6 minutes. Then remove the pizza
from the oven and distribute the
thyme, rosemary, and chives over the
garlic, and cook for another 6 minutes.
Season with salt to taste.

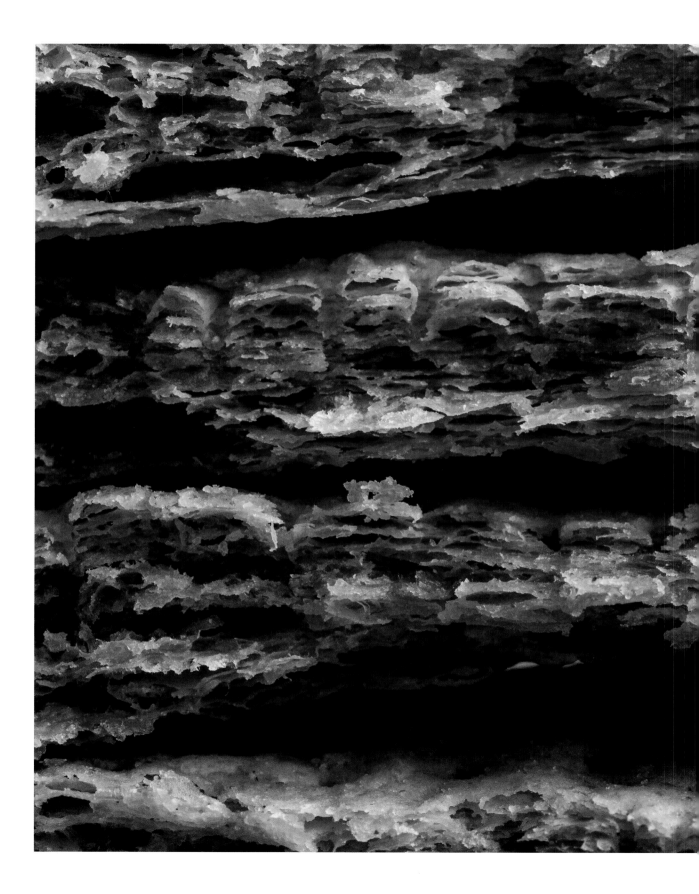

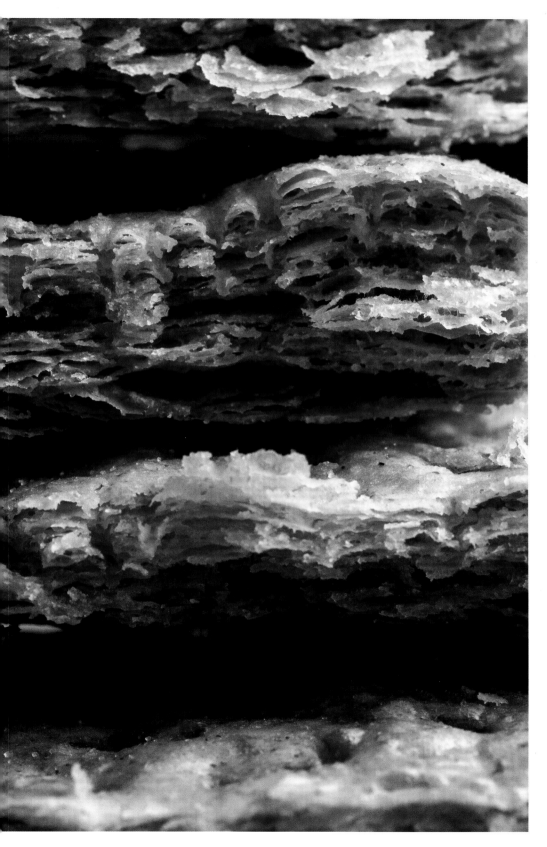

MAKING PASTRY, COOKIES, AND CAKES

While the other chapters in this cookbook tackle self-contained themes—pizza dough, pasta dough, and bread dough—this one covers a wider variety of sweet baked goods, ranging from laminated doughs to cookie doughs to cake batters. These recipes might seem simple, especially for a bread baker who has a total mastery of wheats and flours, but no amount of wheat expertise can save a cookie made with butter that has not been creamed properly. And I know I'm not alone when I say a badly made piece of bread is a lot more satisfying that a cookie that turns to dust when you try to pick it up.

Regardless of whether you are making a croissant or a brownie, there are rules that hold true across genres and techniques, such as the amount of water, or hydration, required for each recipe. All the recipes here specify a greater quantity of liquid than the same recipe would require if made with commercial flour. And while we are on the topic of ingredients, a word about sugar: one of the trends I have noticed among bakers who work with unsifted, freshly milled flour is a conservative approach to sugar. I assume the impulse is driven by a desire to make the dessert healthier or to put the flavor of the wheat in the front row. I have always been of the mind-set that if you are going to sink, you'd might as well drown, so if I am going to use sugar, I use it to its full potential. Indeed, when mixing sugar with freshly milled flour—especially flavor-packed rye—a magical thing happens: you turn the flour's already intense flavor volume up to 11.

CHOOSING THE RIGHT GRAIN FOR THE JOB

While flavor often guides my choice of wheat, the final grain selection must also provide the structural characteristics I am looking for, such as strength or extensibility. For example, when you make laminated doughs, you need a wheat that is strong enough to "lock" the butter into the dough layers while also offering extensibility so you can roll out the dough without it cracking. You can achieve this either by choosing a wheat like Warthog that has both strength and extensibility or by blending flours like Kansas Turkey wheat with Sonora or Frederick to combine these desired characteristics. Based purely on their structural potential, soft wheat flours like Sonora and Frederick are better for delicate cakes or cookies.

MILLING FOR PASTRY, COOKIES, AND CAKES

When milling for cakes and pastries, run the stones as close together as possible so you get a really fine powder to enhance the softness of the resulting dough. You can back the stones off and do a coarser grind when milling for cookies, which can be more rustic in texture.

EXTRACTION

Due to bran's "sharp" edges, which break down pastry dough, the flours in this chapter's recipes should be as close as possible to 30% inclusion (see page 30), achieved by sifting the flour through a fine-mesh sieve (see page 60) or, if you have it, a 100-micron screen. The whole wheat croissants' bread-like doughy components favor full bran inclusion because the bran acts like a knife and cuts the gluten structure, which gives you a more delicate pastry. Cookie doughs and cake batters that include creamed butter are more forgiving when it comes to higher inclusions of bran because although the butter shortens the gluten network, the recipe doesn't rely on gluten development to the extent that bread does.

When sifting, reserve the soft bran of Sonora wheat to use in puff pastry. Adding softer bran to pastry gives it a nice texture, and the bran's edges are less sharp, cutting up the dough structure less than hard bran would.

MIXING

Mixing times tend to be longer for recipes using fresh-milled flour than for recipes that call for commodity flour. You don't have to be as concerned with overmixing a cake batter made with unsifted flour because the bran content shortens the gluten strands, which naturally makes the final product more tender. It also takes more time to mix sugar into the dough evenly.

FERMENTING

Of the dozen recipes in this chapter, only the Whole Wheat Croissants (page 221) contain yeast and levain. The dough is fermented overnight in the refrigerator. During the fermentation process, the dough becomes stronger, which helps it lock in the butter during lamination. It also contributes to the dough's flavor. Because the other doughs and batters in the chapter do not ferment, I choose strongly flavored wheats for them.

BAKING

Pastry made with freshly milled flour always takes a longer time to bake than the same recipe prepared with commodity wheat because the density of the flour components is more complex for freshly milled flour. White flour, which lacks bran or germ, cooks more quickly than stone-milled flour. I find that increasing the baking time specified in a commodity flour recipe by 20% does the trick. These recipes account for the difference, of course, but you can generally apply this principle to Grandma's chocolate cake or whatever else you love.

AGING

Follow the instructions in each recipe for unmolding and slicing. Doing either prematurely compromises the structure of the pastry.

PUFF PASTRY

MAKES ABOUT 1¼ KILOGRAMS PUFF PASTRY

This is a very versatile recipe and I use it whenever a craving for flaky pastry hits or a recipe calls for it. For savory needs, I use it for vol-au-vent pastry shells and as a base for vegetable tarts. When I make a cream and pastry–layered Italian dessert called *millefoglie*, I roll the dough a bit thinner than I do for savory dishes, and then I use a docking wheel or a fork to pierce the surface, which makes the pastry "puff" more evenly. Because puff pastry is laminated, I need a strong flour to "hold in" the butter between the layers I create by rolling and folding. Sonora or another soft wheat flour ensures the delicate texture characteristic of this pastry. The dough is refrigerated overnight, so begin the puff pastry the day before you plan to bake it.

455 grams unsalted butter, chilled to 38°F to 42°F

260 grams cold water

150 grams soft spring wheat flour (I like Sonora)

310 grams hard winter wheat flour (I like Warthog)

50 grams bran (I like Sonora)

11 grams sea salt

5 grams lemon juice

5 grams malt syrup

Bench flour, for dusting (see tip on page 138)

Cut 100 grams of the butter into ½-inch cubes. In the bowl of a stand mixer fitted with the dough hook, combine the water, the soft spring wheat flour, hard winter wheat flour, bran, butter cubes, salt, lemon juice, and malt syrup. Mix on low speed until the flour is incorporated, about 3 minutes. Cover the bowl with plastic wrap and set it aside to let the dough rest at room temperature for 1 hour.

With a bench scraper, loosen the dough from the sides of the bowl and turn it out onto a work surface lightly dusted with bench flour. With a rolling pin, pound the dough into a rectangle measuring 26 × 8 inches and ½ inch thick. Place the dough on a parchment-lined baking sheet, cover it with plastic wrap, and transfer it to the refrigerator to chill for 30 minutes.

MEANWHILE, PREPARE THE BUTTER BLOCK: With the bench scraper, cut the remaining 355 grams butter into 1-inch-thick pats (1) Place the pats between two sheets of parchment paper (2) and, using a rolling pin, pound the butter into a rectangle measuring 13 × 8 inches and ½ inch thick (3). Trim the edges (4) and incorporate the trimmings into the butter block (5) until you have the desired rectangle (6). If necessary, grip the short ends of the parchment and drag the butter block back and forth over the edge of a countertop to make it more pliable (7) and keep rolling (8). Transfer the butter block to the refrigerator and chill until cold, about 20 minutes.

(recipe continues through page 219)

Transfer the dough to a work
surface well-floured with bench
flour with one long side facing you.
Place the butter block in the center
of the rolled-out dough (9) and
fold the two outer quarters of the
dough over it like an open book (10).
With the rolling pin, roll the surface
of the dough all over (11). Flip the
dough and repeat on the other side.
Flip once more, so the dough is
seam-side up. Working in only one
direction, begin rolling the dough
from the center away from you (12).
Turn it 180 degrees and repeat.

With one short edge closest to you, fold the top third of the dough toward the middle (13), and then the bottom third up to the folded edge (14, 15). Then fold the dough in half (16, 17). Press your finger into the bottom right corner to make a dimple so you can track your turns and folds. Transfer the dough to a baking sheet, cover it with plastic wrap, and refrigerate until cold, about 20 minutes.

Put the dough on a well-floured work surface with the dimple at the bottom right corner (18). With a rolling pin, roll the surface of the dough all over. Flip the dough and repeat on the other side (19). Flip once more. Working in one direction only, begin rolling the dough from the center away from you (20). Turn it 180 degrees and repeat. With one long edge closest to you, fold the righthand third toward the middle (21), and then the lefthand third over the folded part, brushing away any excess flour (22). Press two fingers into the bottom right corner to make two dimples to indicate two turns. Transfer the dough to a baking sheet, cover it with plastic wrap, and refrigerate until cool, about 20 minutes.

Repeat the pounding, rolling, turning, folding, dimpling, and chilling sequence 2 more times. Refrigerate the dough overnight. (Wrapped in plastic wrap, the dough will keep for up to 3 days in the refrigerator or up to 4 weeks in the freezer.)

Preheat the oven to 425°F.

Place the dough on a well-floured surface and roll it out to a thickness of ½ inch. Cut the dough into pieces that fit your needs and transfer the pieces to parchment-lined baking sheets. Bake until browned, about 35 minutes.

Stored in a brown paper bag or wrapped in plastic wrap, puff pastry keeps well for up to 3 days on the counter; or wrapped in plastic wrap, it will keep in the refrigerator for up to 1 week or in the freezer for up to 6 months.

WHOLE WHEAT CROISSANTS

MAKES 24 CROISSANTS

Croissants might seem daunting, considering all the steps involved in making a flaky, layered pastry, but they are also rewarding to master. Like everything else in life, practice makes perfect. I guarantee, even if your first few tries aren't stellar, no taste tester is going to let your practice runs go to waste! I always make croissants with hard winter wheat flour and I never sift it; the bran and germ give the pastry tremendous flavor. However, the sharp edges of milled bran break down the dough's structure, so whole wheat flour is harder to work with. To build up to a whole wheat dough, I recommend practicing first with lower-bran-inclusion flour: sift out all the bran, then add 10% back to the flour, increasing the bran amount by 10% each time until you reach 100% whole wheat flour.

Because whole wheat flour includes so much bran, the dough is thirstier than one made with less bran, so listen to the dough, adding a bit more water if needed to hydrate the dough (and less while practicing with smaller bran amounts). Whole wheat fresh-milled dough is more delicate and harder to fold than an all-purpose-flour version, so I usually shoot for two or three folds during the lamination phase versus around six. The dough is twice refrigerated overnight, so begin the recipe 2 days before you plan to bake the croissants.

VARIATION

Use 700 grams hard winter wheat flour (I like Kansas Turkey) and 300 grams soft white wheat flour (I like Sonora or Frederick). This blend of strong hard winter wheat and delicate soft white wheat balances structure and tenderness.

280 grams unsalted butter, chilled to 38°F to 42°F

270 grams cold water

250 grams whole milk

80 grams beaten eggs

150 grams sugar

1,000 grams hard winter wheat flour (I like Warthog), plus more for dusting

4 grams fresh compact yeast

22 grams sea salt

140 grams Levain (page 90)

1 whole egg, beaten

Covering the croissants with an inverted box while they rise will prevent the dough from drying out. The box also maintains a constant temperature around the croissants and keeps its distance from the dough to allow it to ferment uninhibited.

(recipe continues through page 223)

Cut 40 grams of the butter into ½-inch cubes. In the bowl of a stand mixer fitted with the dough hook, combine the water, the milk, the 80 grams eggs, the butter cubes, and the sugar, flour, and yeast. Mix on low speed until the flour is incorporated, about 4 minutes. Cover the bowl with plastic wrap and place the dough in the refrigerator to ferment for 8 hours or overnight.

Uncover the bowl. Add the salt and the levain, and mix on medium speed for 2 minutes to incorporate. Use a thermometer to test the dough: it should be 75°F to 77°F, slightly cooler than your hands. If it is not, move the dough to a warmer part of your kitchen until it reaches the desired temperature range. Cover the bowl with plastic wrap and place the dough in the refrigerator to ferment once more for 8 hours or overnight. (Wrapped in plastic wrap, the fermented dough will keep for up to 1 day in the refrigerator or up to 4 weeks in the freezer.)

With a bench scraper, loosen the dough from the sides of the bowl and turn it out onto a work surface lightly dusted with flour. With a rolling pin, pound the dough into a rectangle measuring 26 × 9 inches and ½ inch thick. Place the dough on a parchment-lined baking sheet, cover it with plastic wrap, and transfer it to the refrigerator to chill for 30 minutes.

MEANWHILE, PREPARE THE BUTTER BLOCK: With a bench scraper, cut the remaining 240 grams chilled butter into 1-inch-thick pats. Place the pats between two sheets of parchment paper and, using a rolling pin, pound the butter into a rectangle measuring approximately 11 × 8 inches and ½ inch thick. Trim the edges and incorporate the trimmings into the butter block until you have the desired rectangle. If necessary, grip the short ends of the parchment and drag the butter block back and forth over the edge of a countertop to make it more pliable. Transfer the butter block to the refrigerator and chill until cold, about 20 minutes.

With the bench scraper, loosen the dough from the sides of the bowl and turn it out onto a lightly floured surface. With a rolling pin, roll the dough into a rectangle measuring approximately 13 × 18 inches. Place the butter block in the center of the rolled-out dough and fold the two outer quarters of the dough over it like an open book. Transfer the folded dough to a parchment-lined baking sheet and place it in the refrigerator, covered with plastic wrap, to chill for 30 minutes.

Transfer the dough to a heavily floured work surface. With the rolling pin, working in only one direction, begin rolling the dough from the center away from you. Turn it 180 degrees and repeat. Work the dough into a ¼-inch-thick

slab, keeping it in a rectangular shape measuring 26 × 9 inches. With one short edge closest to you, fold the top third of the dough toward the middle, and the bottom third over the folded part (like folding a business letter). Then fold the dough in half. Transfer the folded dough to the baking sheet and chill it in the refrigerator, covered, for 30 minutes. Then repeat the rolling, folding, and chilling steps.

SHAPE THE CROISSANTS: Roll the dough out to measure 18 × 24 inches, and use a sharp knife to slice it in half lengthwise into two 9 × 24-inch rectangles. Then slice each piece into isosceles triangles with 4-inch bases and 9-inch sides.

Cut a 1-inch-deep slit into each 4-inch base. Starting at the cut end, roll the pastry into a loose roll. Place the rolls tip down on two parchment-lined baking sheets. Cover each baking sheet with an inverted box and set them aside at room temperature until the dough has increased in volume by 30%, about 2 hours.

Preheat the oven to 425°F.

Brush the croissants with the remaining beaten egg. Bake for 15 minutes; then reduce the heat to 350°F and bake until they are a deep golden brown and airy, about 30 minutes. Serve immediately.

SHORTBREAD COOKIES

MAKES 12 SHORTBREAD COOKIES

Shortbread was the first cookie I fell in love with. Bruce Rascher, my boss at Henry VIII roast beef shop in Portland, Maine, made a Scottish shortbread that was addictive. At age eighteen, I became obsessed with re-creating it, and this recipe is the result—just fifteen years later! By definition, shortbread cookies are made of equal parts butter and flour, so they are quite fragile and temperature is very important when making the dough. The butter has to stay super-cold to provide structure for the dough, while the flour has to be very strong to "lock in" the butter. I choose durum wheat flour here to provide the structure the shortbread needs. The Iraq durum has lots of protein but low starch quality, so I add rice flour to balance these characteristics.

VARIATION

Give your shortbread even more flavor by mixing flax, sesame, or sunflower seeds into the dough.

500 grams unsalted butter

100 grams heavy cream

225 grams sugar

500 grams durum flour (I like Iraq), plus more for dusting

100 grams Rice Flour (page 74)

9 grams sea salt, plus more for sprinkling

Place the butter in a small saucepan set over low heat and cook slowly until it browns, about 45 minutes.

Transfer the browned butter to the bowl of a stand mixer and refrigerate it, uncovered, until cooled, about 20 minutes.

Add the cream and sugar to the cool browned butter, and beat with the paddle attachment on high speed until the mixture is light and airy, about 4 minutes.

Meanwhile, whisk together the durum flour, rice flour, and salt in a medium bowl. Add this mixture all at once to the beaten butter mixture, and beat on low speed just until the dough comes together, about 1 minute.

With a bench scraper, loosen the dough from the sides of the bowl and turn it out onto a lightly floured surface. Form it into a block measuring roughly 12 × 8 inches. Wrap the block in parchment paper and refrigerate until chilled, about 30 minutes.

Meanwhile, preheat the oven to 325°F. Line two baking sheets with parchment paper.

Unwrap the block of dough, cut it in half lengthwise, and slice each half into six 2 × 4-inch pieces. Place the cookies on the prepared baking sheets, spacing them at least ¼ inch apart. Sprinkle them with a little sea salt and bake just until golden, 11 to 13 minutes.

Set the cookies aside to cool on a wire rack for 1 hour before serving. The cookies will keep in an airtight container at room temperature for up to 2 weeks, or in an airtight container in the freezer for up to 6 months.

SHORTBREAD PIE CRUST

MAKES TWO 9-INCH PIE CRUSTS

This recipe adapts the shortbread cookie recipe to make two pie shells. It's not a classic pie crust, but it's easy to pull together, is a tasty way to use freshly milled flour, and is versatile enough to go with varied fillings, from peaches to lemon curd to chocolate. For a tender crust, I use Magog, which is a very weak flour, and buckwheat, which doesn't have any gluten. The buckwheat also lends flavor to the rather bland Magog. Magog is delicious when it's fermented, but it's in this recipe for the structure. You'll have to bake the crust first before filling it.

500 grams unsalted butter, plus more for greasing

225 grams sugar

500 grams Magog flour

100 grams buckwheat flour, plus more for dusting

9 grams sea salt

50 grams ice water

———————————

Before baking the pie crust, place parchment paper over the raw dough and distribute dried beans over the surface. This will keep the dough from rising and warping in the dish as it bakes.

Place the butter in a small saucepan set over low heat and cook slowly until it browns, about 45 minutes.

Transfer the browned butter to the bowl of a stand mixer and refrigerate it, uncovered, until cooled, about 20 minutes.

Add the sugar to the cool browned butter and beat with the paddle attachment on high speed until the mixture is light and airy, about 4 minutes.

Meanwhile, whisk together the Magog flour, buckwheat flour, and salt in a medium bowl. Add this mixture all at once to the beaten butter mixture and beat on low speed just until the dough comes together, about 1 minute. Add the ice water and mix until well incorporated.

Use a bench scraper to loosen the dough from the sides of the bowl, and turn it out onto a parchment-covered work surface. Cut the dough in half and roll each piece between two lightly floured sheets of parchment paper, forming disks about 11 inches in diameter and ⅛ inch thick. Transfer each disk to a greased and floured 9-inch pie dish, gently pressing it into the edges and up the sides. Repair any tears. Refrigerate, uncovered, until firm, about 30 minutes.

Meanwhile, preheat the oven to 350°F.

With a fork, poke holes all over the surface of the crusts. Use dried beans on parchment to weight down the raw pie crusts as they bake. Bake until golden brown, about 20 minutes.

The pie crusts are now ready to be baked again with your choice of filling.

CHOCOLATE CHIP COOKIES

MAKES 32 COOKIES

Chocolate chip cookies are an American classic and we all have our favorite recipe. At the Brooklyn Bread Lab, we were really driven to make the most memorable cookie our guests had ever eaten. After many trials, we finally arrived at a rye-based dough, which we loved for the way the flavorful rye tasted with the butter and chocolate. The recipe uses raw sugar in order to keep with the natural wholesomeness of the flour, and I add a bit of muscovado sugar as well. Together, these sweeteners bring the rye flavor in this cookie to a whole new level. The recipe uses whole rye, so there is no need to sift the flour.

VARIATION

Customize the flavor of your chocolate chip cookies by adding ground walnuts, fennel seeds, or ground cumin, to name a few possible flavors.

500 grams unsalted butter, softened

500 grams turbinado sugar, such as Sugar in the Raw

350 grams muscovado sugar

15 grams vanilla bean, halved lengthwise and seeds scraped out and reserved

570 grams rye flour

12 grams sea salt

12 grams baking soda

100 grams whole eggs plus 66 grams yolks

625 grams chocolate chips (see tip)

I suggest using the best quality chocolate you can afford. I like to buy blocks of chocolate that is between 64% and 72% cacao, which complements the sweetness of the cookie with its bitterness and offers a nice marriage of fermented cacao flavor with the rye. To make chocolate "chips," simply chop up the block with a heavy knife.

In the bowl of a stand mixer fitted with the paddle attachment, combine the butter, turbinado sugar, muscovado sugar, and vanilla seeds. Cream on high speed until the mixture is light and airy, about 4 minutes.

In a medium bowl, whisk together the flour, salt, and baking soda. With the mixer running on high speed, add the dry ingredients to the butter mixture, a little bit at a time, scraping down the sides of the bowl with each addition. Continue beating on high speed until the batter is light and airy, about 5 minutes.

In a medium bowl, whisk together the whole eggs and the yolks. With the mixer running on medium speed, add the egg mixture to the dough a little bit at a time, scraping down the sides of the bowl with each addition. Beat until the eggs are incorporated, about 2 minutes, then

reduce the speed to low and stir in the chocolate chips.

Turn the dough out onto a sheet of parchment paper, wrap it up, and refrigerate until chilled, about 30 minutes.

Preheat the oven to 350°F. Line two baking sheets with parchment paper.

Using a 3-ounce ice cream scoop and spacing the cookies at least ½ inch apart, scoop the dough onto the prepared baking sheets. Bake until golden, 11 to 14 minutes.

Set aside to cool on a wire rack for 30 minutes before serving. The cookies will keep in a sealed airtight container at room temperature for up to 2 weeks and in the freezer for up to 6 months.

PIE CRUST

MAKES ONE 12-INCH PIE CRUST

There isn't a huge difference between a crust you would use for a sweet dessert and one you would make for a savory tart, so I use this recipe whether I'm making a peach pie or a classic quiche. In both cases, the crusts should be flaky yet sturdy enough to hold their contents. I choose a soft spring wheat flour because it's light in flavor, easy to work with, and just delicate enough to let the filling shine through. Frederick is a personal favorite for the elegant structure it imparts.

400 grams soft spring wheat flour (I like Frederick), plus more for dusting

15 grams sugar

5 grams sea salt

160 grams cold unsalted butter, cut into ¼-inch cubes, plus more for greasing

80 grams solid vegetable shortening, chilled

130 grams ice water

You want the butter to be ice-cold for this recipe. It needs to keep its integrity to provide structure to the crust. If the butter melts, the crust loses its structure and breaks down. A fun trick is to freeze the butter and then use the large holes on a box grater to grate it. If, while you're working it, the mixture starts to melt, transfer it to a bowl and refrigerate until it rehardens.

In a large bowl, whisk together the flour, sugar, and salt. Add the butter cubes and stir to coat. Turn the mixture out onto a work surface, and with the heel of your hand, press the cold butter into the flour, smearing until the ingredients are incorporated and a shaggy dough forms. Add the shortening and squeeze the dough until smooth, taking care not to melt the fats with the heat of your hand. If necessary, return the dough to the bowl and chill it in the refrigerator for 10 minutes, then continue working.

Transfer the dough back to the large bowl and add 65 grams of the ice water. With your hands, knead the dough as quickly as possible to avoid melting the fats and overworking the dough. If the dough doesn't come together, add the remaining ice water a little bit at a time, mixing to incorporate. (You may not need all the water.) The dough should be smooth and compact. Transfer the bowl to the refrigerator to chill, uncovered, for 1 hour.

Lightly grease a 12-inch fluted tart pan or springform pan. Place the dough between two lightly floured sheets of parchment paper, and with a rolling pin, roll it into a disk about 15 inches in diameter and ⅛ inch thick. Transfer the dough to the prepared pan, gently pressing it into the edges and up the sides; if you're using a springform pan, the dough should come about ¾ inch up the sides. Repair any tears. Refrigerate, uncovered, until firm, about 30 minutes.

Meanwhile, preheat the oven to 350°F.

With a fork, poke holes all over the surface of the crust. Use dried beans on parchment to weight down the raw pie crust as it bakes (see tip on page 227). Bake until golden brown, about 20 minutes.

The pie crust is now ready to be baked again with your choice of filling.

SPONGE CAKE

MAKES TWO 8-INCH CAKE LAYERS

When I was living in Italy, *pan di Spagna*, also known as sponge cake, was the go-to party food. At every birthday or otherwise celebratory event, there would be a layered sponge cake frosted with whipped cream. For me, this cake is the epitome of simplicity and satisfaction. When I began my cake journey—a real detour from my savory kitchen expertise—I knew that sponge cake would be the ideal vehicle for showcasing wheat in its purest form. Frederick soft wheat provides the light structure essential for a great sponge cake, as well as the great wheat flavor I was going for here. It has just enough flavor to really show through, balancing against the egginess of the cake.

VARIATIONS

- Add 40 grams of cacao powder to the batter to make a chocolate cake.

- Layer the cake with fresh fruit or jam.

15 eggs, separated

456 grams sugar, plus more for dusting the pan

7 grams vanilla bean, halved lengthwise, seeds scraped out and reserved

3 grams cream of tartar

3 grams sea salt

170 grams soft white wheat flour (I like Frederick)

Whipped Cream (recipe follows)

WHIPPED CREAM

MAKES 6 CUPS

700 grams heavy cream

100 grams sugar

4 grams (1 teaspoon) pure vanilla extract

In a large, chilled stainless-steel bowl, whip together the cream, sugar, and vanilla with a hand mixer until stiff peaks form. Use immediately.

Preheat the oven to 375°F. Line two 8-inch springform cake pans with parchment paper.

In the bowl of a stand mixer fitted with the whisk attachment, whip the egg yolks and 228 grams of the sugar on medium speed until fluffy, 4 to 6 minutes, then set aside in a separate large bowl.

Thoroughly clean the bowl and whisk attachment of the stand mixer, then whip the egg whites and vanilla seeds on medium speed until frothy, about 30 seconds. In a separate medium bowl, whisk together the remaining 228 grams sugar, the cream of tartar, and salt. Raise the speed of the mixer to medium-high and add the dry mixture to the egg whites a little bit at a time. Beat to medium-soft peaks, 4 to 6 minutes. Set aside.

Sift the flour directly into the yolk mixture. Using a rubber spatula, fold in the flour to incorporate it, and then carefully fold in the egg white mixture.

Pour the batter into the prepared pans, dividing it evenly. Bake until the cakes are lightly browned, the center springs back when pressed, and a tester comes out clean, about 40 minutes. (Begin checking the cakes for doneness at the 30-minute mark.)

Set the cakes aside to cool slightly on a wire rack for 10 minutes before unmolding. Then release the cakes from their springform pans and allow them to cool completely, about 45 minutes.

Discard the parchment, and then frost the stacked cakes all over with the whipped cream, dividing it evenly between the layers, top, and sides. The frosted layer cake will keep in an airtight container in the refrigerator for up to a week.

CARROT CAKE

MAKES TWO 8-INCH CAKE LAYERS

This carrot cake uses Sonora soft wheat, which accentuates the carrot flavor, almost seasoning the carrot. The recipe also includes my pal chef Alberto Maggi's secret ingredient, grapefruit puree, a touch he adds to many of his sweets at Osteria della Brughiera to kick them up a notch.

Unsalted butter, for greasing

30 grams honey

100 grams walnut oil

100 grams coconut oil

100 grams Grapefruit Puree (page 239)

225 grams cane sugar

15 grams ground cinnamon

3½ grams sea salt

170 grams soft white wheat flour (I like Sonora), plus more for dusting

3½ grams baking soda

7½ grams cream of tartar

250 grams carrots, grated

115 grams walnuts, finely chopped

100 grams shredded coconut

142 grams eggs, beaten

Cream Cheese Frosting (recipe follows)

Preheat the oven to 350°F. Grease and flour two 8-inch springform cake pans.

In a large bowl, mix the honey, walnut oil, coconut oil, grapefruit purée, and cane sugar with a spoon until incorporated. In a separate large bowl, whisk together the cinnamon, salt, flour, baking soda, and cream of tartar. Add the carrots, walnuts, and shredded coconut to the flour mixture, and stir until incorporated. Add the carrot mixture to the honey mixture, stirring until incorporated. Gradually stir in the eggs until incorporated.

Pour the batter into the prepared pans, dividing it evenly. Bake until a tester comes out clean, about 45 minutes. (Begin checking the cakes for doneness at the 30-minute mark.)

Set the cakes aside to cool completely on a wire rack for 30 minutes before unmolding. Then release the cakes from their springform pans, and frost the stacked cakes all over with the cream cheese frosting, dividing it evenly between the layers, top, and sides. The frosted layer cake will keep in an airtight container in the refrigerator for up to a week.

CREAM CHEESE FROSTING

MAKES ABOUT 4 CUPS

452 grams cream cheese, softened

Grated zest of 1 lemon

Grated zest of 1 orange

3 grams vanilla bean, halved lengthwise, seeds scraped out and reserved

226 grams unsalted butter, softened

226 grams confectioners' sugar

In the bowl of a stand mixer fitted with the paddle attachment, cream the cream cheese on low speed until it is smooth and aerated, about 4 minutes. Scrape down the sides of the bowl and the paddle, and then add the lemon zest, orange zest, and vanilla seeds. Continue mixing on low speed, adding the butter a little bit at a time and scraping down the sides of the bowl with each addition, until it is all incorporated. Add the confectioners' sugar and mix until incorporated, about 30 seconds. Beat the mixture on high speed until it is fluffy and aerated, about 2 minutes.

Stored in a sealed container, the frosting will keep in the refrigerator for up to 1 week.

MUFFINS

MAKES 18 MUFFINS

It wasn't until I hit my thirties that I started eating breakfast. Once upon a time, I could survive on coffee alone. Now that those days are over, I bake barely sweet and very tender muffins for myself. They remind me of unfrosted cupcakes. To get that cakey texture I'm after, I use soft spring wheat flour. On its own, the flour would make a really soft but rather bland muffin. So to impart a savory note—not to mention loads of nutrition—I add plenty of bran. The resulting muffin is a delicious and nourishing way to start the day and it's fun to flavor the batter with dried or fresh fruit, depending on what I fancy that day.

VARIATIONS

- Add around 1,200 grams of blueberries, chocolate chips, walnuts, or raisins.

- I also enjoy combining 900 grams of dried sour cherries and 300 grams of currants.

Unsalted butter, for greasing

475 grams soft spring wheat flour (I like Sonora), plus more for dusting

280 grams light brown sugar

178 grams bran (I like Sonora)

22½ grams baking soda

11 grams baking powder

5½ grams ground cinnamon

5 grams sea salt

590 grams buttermilk

200 grams eggs

185 grams extra-virgin olive oil

100 grams molasses

45 grams honey

5 grams pure vanilla extract

Streusel (recipe follows)

Preheat the oven to 395°F. Butter and flour 18 cups in muffin tins.

In the bowl of a stand mixer fitted with the paddle attachment, combine the soft spring wheat flour, light brown sugar, bran, baking soda, baking powder, cinnamon, and salt.

In a separate large bowl, mix together the buttermilk, eggs, olive oil, molasses, honey, and vanilla.

With the mixer running on medium speed, add the wet ingredients to the flour mixture, a little bit at a time, scraping down the sides of the bowl with each addition. Continue beating until all the ingredients are incorporated.

Spoon about 225 grams of the batter into each prepared muffin cup. Sprinkle the streusel over the batter, distributing it evenly. Bake until a tester comes out clean, about 40 minutes. (Begin checking the muffins for doneness at the 30-minute mark.) The muffins will keep in a sealed airtight container at room temperature for up to 1 week.

STREUSEL

MAKES 500 GRAMS (2¼ CUPS)

125 grams sugar

125 grams sanding sugar

80 grams soft spring wheat flour (I like Sonora)

50 grams bran

1½ grams ground coriander

1 gram ground allspice

120 grams unsalted butter, cold

In a medium bowl, combine the sugar, sanding sugar, flour, bran, coriander, and allspice. With a bench scraper, cut in the butter until incorporated.

BROWNIES

MAKES 24 BROWNIES

I serve bite-size brownies as part of my *piccola pasticceria* plate, the Italian equivalent of petit fours, which signals the end of a fine-dining meal. They stand up well next to gelées, mini-tarts, and other sweets popular in Italy, and deliver powerful flavor in small doses. In considering brownies' natural tendency to be cloying or a bit fudgy, I chose a flour that would balance out those characteristics and settled on rye. Because rye has low protein, I increased the number of eggs I would normally use in a standard brownie recipe—the whites are rich in protein and they work to improve the texture.

VARIATIONS

- Add chile powder, a variation inspired by chef Laurent Gras—he makes his own mixture of seven different chile varieties for his signature brownies.

- Add a healthy pinch of Chinese five spice, mesquite powder, or ground cinnamon.

- You can also add 450 grams of ground walnuts to the batter.

340 grams unsalted butter, plus more for greasing

910 grams dark chocolate (I like 72% cacao)

560 grams eggs

790 grams sugar

5 grams sea salt

10 grams pure vanilla extract

260 grams rye flour, plus more for dusting

Preheat the oven to 350°F. Grease and flour an 18 × 9-inch baking pan.

In the top of a double boiler set over barely simmering water, melt the butter and chocolate together, stirring constantly until smooth. Keep warm.

In the bowl of a stand mixer fitted with the whisk attachment, whip the eggs, sugar, salt, and vanilla on high speed until the mixture thickens and reaches the ribbon stage, about 8 minutes.

Pour the warm chocolate sauce into the egg mixture and fold to incorporate. Sift the flour directly into the batter and fold to incorporate.

Pour the batter into the prepared baking pan and bake until the surface cracks and a tester comes out clean, 20 to 25 minutes.

Set the pan aside to cool on a wire rack for 40 minutes before slicing and removing the brownies. The brownies will keep in an airtight container at room temperature for up to 10 days.

BISCOTTI

MAKES 36 BISCOTTI

Biscotti are great to serve as part of a dessert cart and to entice people to have an after-dinner drink like Vin Santo, a sweet wine made in Tuscany. My friend Alberto Maggi, a chef at Osteria della Brughiera in Bergamo, used to blend whole bergamots or grapefruits in a blender along with their weight in confectioners' sugar and add the mixture to his biscotti, cakes, and pies—wherever he felt his secret ingredient was needed. He'd even keep a reserve in the freezer for emergencies. The puree has crazy concentrated citrus flavor without adding any bitterness to the finished product, and it imparts tartness and acid, which enhance the sweetness of the biscotti. I use Blue Beard durum here because it has a really pronounced flavor even if it's not fermented and you get a great exotic fruit aroma (like banana!) from the grain. The flavor profile of biscotti evolves over time and reaches its peak on the third day.

250 grams whole raw almonds

500 grams durum flour (I like Blue Beard), plus more for dusting

1 teaspoon baking powder

Pinch of sea salt

300 grams Grapefruit Puree (recipe follows)

4 large eggs

50 grams whole raw pine nuts

Preheat the oven to 350°F.

Place the almonds on a parchment-lined baking sheet and bake for 10 minutes. Allow them to cool until they can be handled, about 20 minutes. Leave the oven on and set the lined baking sheet aside.

In a large bowl, whisk together the flour, baking powder, and salt. In a medium bowl, whisk together the grapefruit puree and the eggs.

Add the cooled almonds and the pine nuts to the flour mixture, and then pour in the egg mixture. Mix with a spoon until the dough comes together. Knead the dough energetically in the bowl with both hands until the almonds and pine nuts are evenly distributed.

With a bench scraper, loosen the dough from the sides of the bowl and turn it out onto a lightly floured surface. Divide the dough in half with the bench scraper. Roll each piece of dough into a log about 4 inches in diameter and about 9 inches long. Place the logs on the reserved lined baking sheet, spacing them at least 2 inches apart. Press them gently to flatten the dough to a uniform height.

Bake until the surface is lightly cracked and a tester comes out clean, 30 minutes. Allow the logs to cool until they can be handled, about 30 minutes. Then cut the logs into approximately ½-inch-thick slices (about 18 pieces each).

Reduce the oven temperature to 300°F. Return the slices to the lined baking sheet and bake for 30 minutes, until the cookies are no longer soft when pressed.

Allow the biscotti to cool completely on the baking sheet, about 20 minutes, before serving. The cookies will keep in an airtight container at room temperature for up to 10 days.

GRAPEFRUIT PUREE

MAKES 450 GRAMS GRAPEFRUIT PUREE

1 medium grapefruit (about 225 grams), unpeeled, seeds removed, coarsely chopped

225 grams confectioners' sugar

Combine the grapefruit chunks and the confectioners' sugar in the bowl of a food processor and pulse until smooth, about 3 minutes.

Stored in a sealed container, the puree will keep for 1 week in the refrigerator and up to 6 months in the freezer.

SCONES

MAKES 12 SCONES

For decades, I have been dedicated to Italian cuisine, so when I was challenged to create a special English-style service for the Williamsburg Hotel, I had to learn the basics. I went on a scone journey through London and interrogated British friends about their mothers' and grandmothers' recipes. I fused these various experiences into my ideal scone, equal parts flaky and tender. Thanks to the Frederick wheat, the scones have a whole lot of wheaty flavor mingling with the butter.

VARIATIONS

- Fold 25 grams of chopped fresh herbs into the mixed dough (3).
- Fold 250 grams of ground nuts or chopped dried fruit into the mixed dough.

900 grams soft spring wheat flour (I like Frederick)

100 grams bran (I like Sonora)

150 grams sugar

25 grams baking soda

18 grams salt

300 grams unsalted butter, cut into ½-inch cubes, chilled

810 grams heavy cream

150 grams turbinado sugar, such as Sugar in the Raw

In a large bowl or on a large work surface, whisk together the flour, bran, sugar, baking soda, and salt. Add the butter cubes and stir to coat (1). With the heel of your hand, press the cold butter into the flour, smearing until the ingredients are incorporated and a shaggy dough forms (2), taking care not to melt the fat with the heat of your hand.

Chill the dough in the refrigerator for 10 minutes. Then add 750 grams of the heavy cream (4), kneading it into the dough until incorporated. Chill for 10 minutes more.

Meanwhile, preheat the oven to 425°F. Line two baking sheets with parchment paper.

With a bench scraper, turn the dough out onto a work surface and divide the dough in half (5). Shape each half into a log 4 inches wide, 2 inches high, and 1 inch thick. Cut the dough into 3 equal pieces, and then cut those pieces in half diagonally to make triangular scones (6). Transfer the pieces to the prepared baking sheets, spacing them at least 1 inch apart. Brush with the remaining 60 grams heavy cream (7) and sprinkle with the turbinado sugar (8). Bake until golden brown, about 35 minutes. The scones will keep in an airtight container at room temperature for up to 1 week.

(recipe continues through page 245)

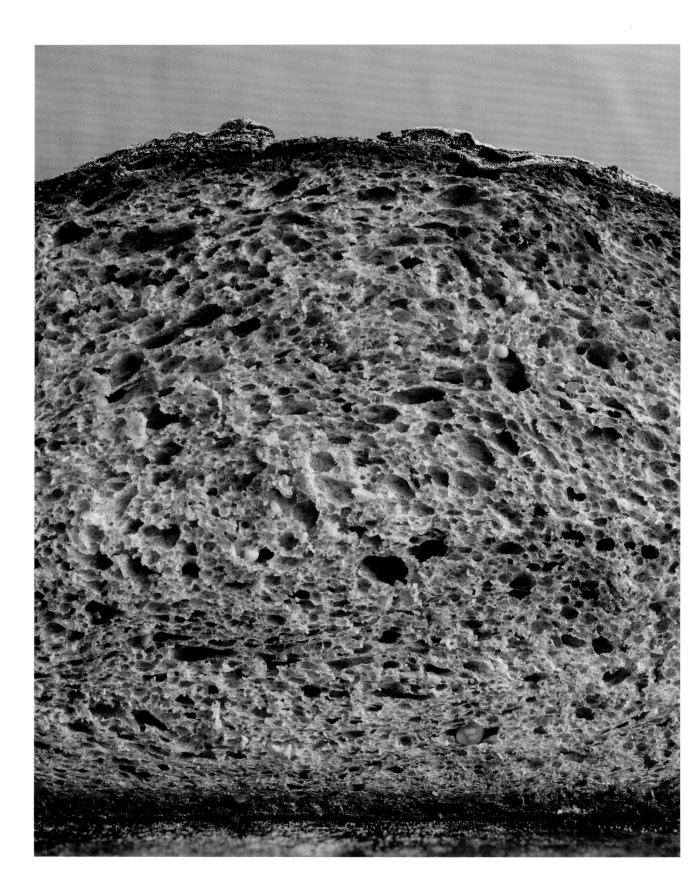

RESOURCES

BOOKS ON BAKING, WHEAT, AND MILLING

Alderson, Erin. *The Homemade Flour Cookbook: The Home Cook's Guide to Milling Nutritious Flours and Creating Delicious Recipes with Every Grain, Legume, Nut, and Seed from A–Z*. Beverly, MA: Fair Winds Press, 2014.

Alterman, Tabitha. *Whole Grain Baking Made Easy: Craft Delicious, Healthful Breads, Pastries, Desserts, and More*. Minneapolis: Voyageur Press, 2015.

Basey, Marleeta F. *Flour Power: A Guide to Modern Home Grain Milling*. Albany, OR: Jermar Press, 2004.

Bertolli, Paul. *Cooking by Hand*. New York: Clarkson Potter, 2003.

Bobrow-Strain, Aaron. *White Bread: A Social History of the Store-Bought Loaf*. Boston: Beacon, 2012.

Calvel, Raymond. *The Taste of Bread*. Translated by Ronald L. Wirtz. New York: Springer, 2013. Originally published as *Le goût du pain* (Les Lilas, France: Éditions Jérôme Villette, 1990).

Egan, Timothy. *The Worst Hard Time: The Untold Story of Those Who Survived the Great American Dust Bowl*. Boston: Mariner Books, 2006.

Grant, Susan McKenna. *Piano, Piano, Pieno: Authentic Food from a Tuscan Farm*. New York: Overlook Press, 2006.

Halloran, Amy. *The New Bread Basket: How the New Crop of Grain Growers, Plant Breeders, Millers, Maltsters, Bakers, Brewers, and Local Food Activists Are Redefining Our Daily Loaf*. White River Junction, VT: Chelsea Green, 2015.

Hamelman, Jeffrey. *Bread: A Baker's Book of Techniques and Recipes*. Hoboken, NJ: Wiley, 2012.

Mallon, Shanna, and Tim Mallon. *The Einkorn Cookbook: Discover the World's Purest and Most Ancient Form of Wheat*. Beverly, MA: Fair Winds Press, 2014.

Wing, Daniel, and Alan Scott. *The Bread Builders: Hearth Loaves and Masonry Ovens*. White River Junction, VT: Chelsea Green, 1999.

MILLS

KoMo Magic Grain Mill
pleasanthillgrain.com/shop-by/brand/komo_mills/

Meadows Mills
800-626-2282
meadowsmills.com

Mockmill
302-310-3230
wolfgangmock.com

MILLERS, WHEAT BERRY, AND FLOUR SOURCES

Anson Mills
803-467-4122
ansonmills.com
Founded to promote South Carolina's landrace rice varieties, Anson Mills now offers a range of stone-milled organic flours including Sonora wheat, Red Fife, einkorn, farro, and rye.

Barton Springs Mill
512-554-5981
bartonspringsmill.com
Barton Springs Mill stone-grinds sustainably grown whole grains near Austin, Texas.

Camas Country Mill
541-225-5640
camascountrymill.com
This Oregon-based mill and bakery stone-mills heritage grains, as well as Edison, which they created with the WSU Bread Lab.

Carolina Ground
carolinaground.com
This mill, based in North Carolina, sells wheat berries and stone-milled flours with a focus on hard and soft red winter wheat, as well as rye.

Castle Valley Mill
215-340-3609
castlevalleymill.com
Stone-milling spelt, farro, rye, and historic Pennsylvania grains in Bucks County.

Farmer Ground Flour
607-387-1007
farmergroundflour.com
This collaboration between millers Greg Russo and Neal Johnston and organic farmer Thor Oechsner provides locally cultivated grains from New York's Hudson Valley milled to order. Their flours are widely available in specialty shops across New York State and in select Whole Foods locations: rye, spelt, einkorn.

Grist & Toll
626-441-7400
gristandtoll.com
Milling hard red, Sonora, spelt, and rye in Pasadena, California.

Hayden Flour Mills
480-557-0031
haydenflourmills.com
Arizona-based Hayden Flour Mills sells flour made from local heritage grains like Sonora soft wheat.

Heartland Mill
800-232-8533
heartlandmill.com
Milling grains from High Plains farmers, Kansas-based Heartland Mill specializes in high-protein wheats like Turkey wheat and durum and ancient grains like rye and spelt.

Maine Grains
207-474-8001
mainegrains.com
Maine Grains offers stone-milled flour and whole wheat berries such as Red Fife, durum, rye, farro, and spelt in select Whole Foods stores in the Northeast.

Small Valley Milling
717-362-9850
smallvalleymilling.com
Stone-milling hard red wheat, soft red wheat, and ancient grains in rural Pennsylvania.

Wild Hive Farm Community Grain Project
845-266-0660
wildhivefarm.com
Wild Hive mills small batches of flour from organic grain purchased from local and regional farmers in New York's Hudson Valley and its environs.

INSTITUTIONS AND CLASSES

Bread Bakers Guild of America
707-935-1468
bbga.org
The Bread Bakers Guild of America is a community of professional bakers, farmers, millers, suppliers, educators, students, home bakers, technical experts, and bakery owners dedicated to promoting artisan baking.

The Bread Lab at Washington State University
360-707-4640
thebreadlab.wsu.edu
Founded by Dr. Stephen S. Jones in 2011, the Bread Lab is a research, development, and educational institute that promotes affordable and nutritious grains for home cooks and professionals.

Maine Grain Alliance
207-272-6844
kneadingconference.com
This organization preserves and promotes grain traditions among farmers, bakers, and families through educational experiences, programs, and conferences.

ACKNOWLEDGMENTS

Even though in many ways I feel as if my career is just starting, I have to credit my eclectic background and my mentors and friends for making this book possible. For without the education and guidance along the way, I wouldn't have been able to begin to understand how to go about changing the pastas, breads, and cakes I love into fresh-milled glory. Thank you to Marc Vetri for trusting me enough to invest in my first little mill. *Grazie alla squadra dell'Osteria della Brughiera per la conoscenza e la passione.* Many recipes are the product of the tireless collaboration and dedicated testing by my friends Jeff Kozlowski and Josh Pickens of the Brooklyn Bread Lab. I am indebted to the profound knowledge and guidance of JD McLelland. I cannot thank Washington State University Bread Lab enough for their incredible contribution to grain culture; I am in awe of your perseverance. *Danke schön*, Sabine Kray, for generously hosting Katie in Berlin and a shout-out to Zach, Karla, and Aziz for letting her crash in NYC and rescuing her from hellacious NJ Transit trips.

Katie and I want to thank our editor and biggest advocate, Amanda Englander, who is as devoted to pizza, pasta, pastry, and bread as we are. Thank you, Joj, for the sandwiches, *vino*, love, and support. We are grateful to Andrew Thomas Lee for his stunning photos. To Pam Yung and Hans Fama, thank you for your thoughtful commentary, feedback, and testing. And finally, thanks to the whole Clarkson Potter team—Stephanie Huntwork, Christine Tanigawa, Heather Williamson, Erica Gelbard, Stephanie Davis, Gabrielle Van Tassel, and our publisher, Aaron Wehner.

INDEX

ABOUT THE AUTHORS

ADAM LEONTI is a Brooklyn-born, Maine-bred chef and baker. He began cooking as a child, preparing meals alongside his Sicilian grandfather and Neapolitan grandmother, and took his first kitchen job at age fourteen. In 2008 he became the chef de cuisine at Vetri, a critically acclaimed Philadelphia institution that won accolades including *Philadelphia* magazine's Best Italian Restaurant, was a James Beard Foundation Award finalist for Outstanding Restaurant, and was included in *Travel + Leisure* magazine's Best Italian Restaurants in the U.S. In 2012, Adam was named one of *Forbes* magazine's prestigious 30 Under 30 professionals in the food and wine industry, as well as an *Eater* Young Gun. In 2015, Adam founded the Brooklyn Bread Lab, a mill and bakery in Bushwick, Brooklyn. Outside of the kitchen, Adam finds inspiration studying his voluminous cookbook collection, which comprises more than one thousand volumes including a favorite, Giuliano Bugialli's *The Fine Art of Italian Cooking*. He is a graduate of the Restaurant School at Walnut Hill College in Philadelphia. His eponymous restaurant, Leonti, opened in Manhattan's Upper West Side in 2018.

KATIE PARLA, a New Jersey native, is a Rome-based food and beverage journalist, culinary guide, and educator. She is the author of the *Saveur* award–winning food and travel site KatieParla.com, *National Geographic's Walking Rome*, and the ebook *Eating & Drinking in Rome*. Katie has written or contributed to more than twenty-five books about Italy and Turkey. Her travel writing, recipes, and food criticism appear in the *New York Times, Food & Wine, Saveur, Australian Gourmet Traveller, The Guardian, Afar, Condé Nast Traveler, Punch*, and *Eater*, and she is the coauthor of the IACP Award–winning cookbook *Tasting Rome: Fresh Flavors and Forgotten Recipes from an Ancient City*. Her first solo title, *Food of the Italian South,* was published by Clarkson Potter in 2019.